Changing Lightbulbs

A journey through anxiety and depression

SUE TREDGET

CAUSEWAY PUBLISHING

Published in Western Australia by
Causeway Publishing
Wembley Downs, WA 6019
Phone: 0422 228 502
Web: www.suetredget.com

First published in Australia 2017
Copyright © Sue Tredget 2017

All rights reserved. No part of this publication may be reproduced, stored in a retrieval system, or transmitted, in any form or by any means without the prior written permission of the publisher, nor be otherwise circulated in any form of binding or cover other than that in which it is published and without a similar condition being imposed on the subsequent purchaser.

 A catalogue record for this book is available from the National Library of Australia

Creator: Sue Tredget
Title: Changing Lightbulbs
ISBN: 978-0-9876171-6-3
ISBN: 978-0-6480901-2-0 (ebook)

Cover design and layout: Rhianna King Creative (www.rhiannaking.com.au)

Disclaimer
All care has been taken in the preparation of the information herein, but no responsibility can be accepted by the publisher or author for any damages resulting from the misinterpretation of this work. All contact details given in this book were current at the time of publication, but are subject to change.

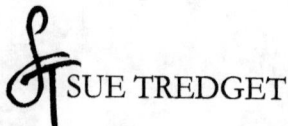

For Ian

Contents

Foreword	ix
Prologue	xi
Introduction	xiii
PART ONE	**1**
Chapter 1	2
Chapter 2	12
Chapter 3	16
Chapter 4	21
Chapter 5	27
Chapter 6	36
Chapter 7	48
Chapter 8	56
Chapter 9	65
PART TWO	**71**
Chapter 10: Finding the thread	72
Chapter 11: Finding balance	78
Chapter 12: Finding creativity and colour	91
Chapter 13: Finding silence	98
Chapter 14: Finding spirituality	107
Chapter 15: Finding yoga	122
Chapter 16: Finding stillness	128
Chapter 17: Finding the way	133
Chapter 18: Finding roots	141
Chapter 19: Finding Ellie	147
Chapter 20: Finding words	160
Chapter 21: Finding childhood	164
Chapter 22: Finding knowledge	172

Chapter 23: Finding friendship	177
Chapter 24: Finding nourishment	184
Chapter 25: Finding acceptance	192
Chapter 26: Beyond busy	206
Chapter 27: Beyond technology	210
Chapter 28: Beyond perfection	224
Chapter 29: Beyond negativity	227
Chapter 30: Beyond blame	232
Chapter 31: Beyond fear	235
Chapter 32: Beyond blue	245
Epilogue	**250**
Acknowledgements	**252**

I believe in miracles
'Cause it's a miracle I'm here
~**Emeli Sandé, Breathing Underwater**

Foreword

Changing Lightbulbs takes us on a journey through Sue Tredget's battle with depression. But the book is far from dark. Sue takes us by the hand and opens her heart in the most delightful of conversations. Like all good conversations, this one is real and raw. It's vulnerable and it's funny. It's honest and it's philosophical.

Sue is no celebrity overcoming her demons in public, no poverty-stricken mother battling in the slums. Rather she's a white, suburban, middle-class mum with a loving husband and great kids. But the very ordinariness of Sue's story is what makes it so compelling. You see, depression does not discriminate. It does not save itself for the famous or the desperate. It strikes wherever it fancies. And, in our modern world, it is striking a lot.

Sue knows there are thousands of others like her – people with seemingly great lives, who feel they don't have the 'right' to depression and who often suffer in silence. She hopes finding the courage to tell her story will help those people realise they are not alone in their suffering, that there's no shame in depression.

But this is no self-help book. It's a simple recounting of one woman's journey from breakdown to breakthrough. It provides a window on a world many of us will experience at some point in our lives. It offers hope for those battling dark times. And, even if you haven't experienced depression, you will recognise the very 'humanness' of Sue's experience. For every life is a grand adventure of highs and lows, of triumphs and tragedies. Every life weaves together a rich tapestry of experiences – both good and bad. Sue's story helps us realise there is hope in the bleakest of times, there is wisdom to be learned from dark days, and that there's beauty on the other side of pain.

I applaud Sue for her bravery in revealing her story.

Samille Mitchell, *Inspired* **Magazine founder**

Prologue

February 2013

It is 3am and my heart is racing, as it does every night now as soon as I lie down. I dread the endless nights, the prospect of hour after hour of sleeplessness, my pulse pounding, thoughts whirling endlessly around my tormented mind. A beating heart should be life affirming, but its frenetic pace only serves to reinforce the pain of living. I don't know where I have gone. I don't know who I am. I don't want to be this person who can't sleep, who doesn't care if she doesn't eat, who stares glassy-eyed at the television screen, willing it to drown out the tormentors in my head. I am here but not here. I don't want to be this person who needs to hide away, who wants to take a giant eraser and rub out all the destructive thoughts, the memories of grief and death and dreadful sadness and betrayal and hurt and anger, but who cannot find one anywhere. I don't want to be this person filled with shame and guilt. Who knows that her children deserve a better mother than this, who is so ashamed of what she has become. I don't want to have to face my husband and know that I must be such a terrible disappointment to him. I no longer recognise myself.

The days are no better. I don't want to move from the sofa where I lie, hour after endless hour, a prisoner in my own head. I don't want to be here. I don't want to live feeling like

I do. I am worthless, a burden, a disappointment, a failure, a shell of the person I used to be not so very long ago. I can't see beyond this time. I can't imagine ever feeling normal again. I can't escape from the cell of my mind.

Make it stop! I scream in silence. *Make it go away*, I implore some unknown deity, *please please please make it all stop*. I am floating somewhere above myself, observing my pathetic body and infected mind. My essence is shrivelled and putrid and of no good to anyone, least of all myself. I am slowly disappearing, spiralling in some deep, dark, nightmarish vortex of despair.

Make it stop.

Introduction

Today in Australia more than one million people are experiencing depression, and more than two million have an anxiety condition. That's a lot of people. One in six women, and one in eight men will experience depression, while one in three women and one in five men are likely to experience anxiety at some point during their lifetime.*

Over the last few years I have been on a mission to discover as much as I can about these common mental health conditions. Depression and anxiety don't discriminate; they can affect people of any age, regardless of social standing, income, profession, post code or circumstance. They can affect people who seem, on the surface, to have absolutely no reason to feel depressed or anxious. I know this because I am one of these people.

I am just an ordinary person. I don't have a public profile or an automatic platform from which to espouse my views on life, and part of me wonders who would possibly want to listen to or read what I have to say. I am very aware that in the global scheme of things I live a privileged life. I have a wonderful family and I live in Western Australia, one of the best places on the planet. What more could a girl want? And what possible reason could I have to feel depressed or anxious? And yet, in February 2013 I fell apart.

Three years on, I consider myself to be recovered, but I am mindful each and every day of just how fragile we are,

---

*Statistics from beyondblue

and of the need to never take our health – both mental and physical – for granted. In March 2015 I joined the *beyondblue* Speaker and Ambassador bureau as a volunteer. Being part of this growing nationwide community working to raise awareness about mental health, and reduce stigma has been beyond rewarding. It is one of the most satisfying things I have ever done. Having the courage to stand up and speak about my experiences, to reach out to others and share my story has been life-changing. I am finding my voice in a society that frequently tells us to keep calm and carry on, to keep going, to pull ourselves together, to put on a brave face, and any number of similar maxims about how we should approach life. But sometimes we aren't able to keep calm, and sometimes we need time before we can carry on. Sometimes we need to come undone before we can put ourselves back together. There should be no shame in that.

While progress is being made in breaking down stigma there is still a way to go. It is widely recognised that those who experience real deprivation, financial hardship and trauma are more prone to depression. We understand and accept that, indeed, we expect it. At the other end of the spectrum, successful Australian women in the media such as Jessica Rowe, who is also a *beyondblue* ambassador, Jane Caro, Magda Szubanski, and people from all walks of life – from politicians to sports men and women – are now becoming more vocal and speaking publicly about their mental health. There seems to be a general acceptance of depression in celebrity quarters, with well-known personalities such as Stephen Fry and Ruby Wax speaking and writing at length about their experiences, and increasing numbers of sports men and women have described their fight with the black dog. This is, of course, a good thing.

But perhaps we are more accepting of the battles of the rich and famous, who live highly public and exposed lives. No wonder depression and anxiety strike them down given the goldfish bowls they often live in, we may think.

But somewhere in the middle, I sense a growing number of people who manage to function and hide their anxiety and depression for a long time. Ordinary people like me, living in the suburbs with mortgages to pay, families to bring up and all the busyness of our modern lives to juggle; people who to the casual observer don't appear to have anything to be depressed or anxious about. And with these ordinary everyday people like me I think there is still a way to go to break down stigma and judgement. We fear that our careers will be affected if we put up our hands and admit to feeling less than OK. We are the people who often remain in denial because the consequences of speaking up just seem too hard to face. This, perhaps, goes some way to explaining the incidence of suicide amongst middle class, hard-working, comfortably-off, seemingly successful people who keep going and keep quiet until death seems to be the only solution. Many people simply don't ask for or get help, often with disastrous consequences. I heard one startling figure which suggested that as many as 75% of people with depression are not accessing the support and treatment they need.

I don't regret having depression and anxiety because they led me to reassess the way I was approaching life. A friend once told me that I didn't have a breakdown, but a breakthrough. At the time I wasn't so sure, but now I see the wisdom in her words. I'd been running on empty for too long and something had to give. My life is more balanced now, less frenetic. I am calmer, more centred and more connected to friends, family, and the wider community. I am learning to embrace and accept my vulnerable and imperfectly human self.

Our culture is one that often seems to value achievement above all else. We feel embarrassed if we make mistakes, we fear the judgement of others, we don't want to be seen as less than perfect. In reality though, a happy, successful life – a good life – is not a life free of pain, failure, suffering or setbacks. These are the things that make us who we are. We need to explode the myth that to be successful or happy we need to live a perfect life. Sometimes the obstacles in our way are the very things that lead us where we want to go.

I'm not a fan of the oft quoted saying: 'Everything happens for a reason.' I find it trite and simplistic. Try telling that to the victims of child abuse or the children of Holocaust survivors. But I was determined that I would create something positive and good from my journey with the black dog and my experience of anxiety, that it would give me a purpose. And it has.

In language teaching we identify the four aspects of communication: listening, reading, writing, and speaking. I am by nature an introvert, and have always been a good listener and an avid reader, but less comfortable voicing my own views. Listening always comes first. As babies we listen to our parents long before we are able to articulate recognisable sounds. As I recovered from my depression I began reading widely about mental health and listening to radio programmes, podcasts and TED talks in which people spoke of their research, their ideas and their experiences in the realm of mental health. Being informed has really helped me to understand what happened to me. It was enormously comforting to discover that I was not alone and that depression and anxiety are in fact very common. They are a part of the human condition. Having bipolar disorder did not stop Isaac Newton from inventing calculus, explaining gravity and building telescopes. Winston Churchill's battles with the black dog did not prevent him from being one of the greatest ever wartime leaders, and Abraham Lincoln managed to lead his country through extremely trying times despite suffering from depression.

My ability to express myself about my own depression and anxiety took time. I took baby steps. I faltered. I chose the wrong forum. Some people didn't want to hear. I kept quiet again for a while. But slowly I began to find my own voice, and while I am still careful about who I tell, I am gradually developing the confidence to speak up.

I have always loved to write. Since childhood I've composed poems and stories and kept diaries. Writing in general comes quite naturally to me. I'm one of the few teachers who actually enjoy writing school reports and I love setting assessments and exams. I love the beauty of the written word, the power of language and the secret intimacy of curling up with a good book. In the aftermath of my breakthrough, I began writing things down. Just thoughts, perceptions and observations, ideas that came to mind, whimsical musings on life. After one of my presentations for *beyondblue* a woman approached me and told me I should write a book. "Funny you should say that," I said, "I've always wanted to write a book."

So here it is. It is not a self-help book, it is not a step-by-step guide to beating depression, it is not a how-to for living with anxiety. There is no one size fits all. Each person's experience will be different, and each person's recovery will follow a different path and timeframe. I am not, and would never claim to be an expert on mental health. I am just a person, like the billions of others on this tiny revolving planet of ours, trying to make sense of my place on it, and this is my story.

PART ONE

lights out

Chapter 1

*I would like more sisters, that the taking out of
one might not leave such stillness.*

~**Emily Dickinson**

So how does a fairly ordinary, unremarkable, fifty-something wife and mother, living in the leafy western suburbs of Perth, Western Australia fall apart? The thing is, mental health problems can happen to anyone. Just ask Prince Harry. After years of silence he has now spoken publicly about the effect his mother's death had on his mental health, saying that he wishes he'd done it much earlier. He, William and Kate have now joined forces to a launch their Heads Together campaign, with the aim of bringing attitudes to mental health in the UK into line with the way physical health is viewed, and change the conversation from one of 'fear and stigma to one of support and openness.' Mental health problems can affect anyone, even members of the Royal Family says Harry. And he's right. It can affect anyone, even people who seem, on the surface, to have absolutely no reason to be depressed or anxious. I know this because it happened to me. And when it happened to me it hit me with such force that I was left, quite literally, gasping for breath. For a while, I thought I would never recover. I thought my life was over. I couldn't see a time when I would make it out of the tunnel and into the light.

When I fell apart I was at work having a conversation with a colleague, something to do with the importance of integrating more technology into the classroom. Well it wasn't really a conversation. She was talking and I was slowly dying. I remember standing in the school courtyard with the strangest sensation of somehow disappearing into myself. Everything went into slow motion, the background voices of the students began to fade. I remember looking at my colleague's face and seeing her lips move but not having any idea what she was saying. I could hear the words but they made no sense. My colleague meant well; my colleague did not cause my collapse. But that moment is clearly etched in my memory. She must have been horrified as she watched me disintegrate.

In the aftermath of my meltdown, I took some time off work to recover. The problem was that I was unaware of just how much time I needed. Despite my collapse I was, to a large extent, still in denial at how overwhelmed I had become. I have since learned that feeling overwhelmed seems to be an increasingly common phenomenon in our modern workplaces where constant improvement and feedback are king.

What is it about feedback these days? Everything has to been analysed and quantified and pulled apart. We are expected to be in a permanent state of improving, reviewing and renewing, always changing and growing and trying new things. That all sounds very nice and perfectly reasonable, I hear you say. Change is good, of course. Innovation is great, no one would argue with that, but how about a bit of consolidation for a change? How about just focusing on teaching as well as we can instead of jumping on the next bandwagon, which inevitably involves a whole pile of paperwork and administration.

It's exhausting, being in a continual state of improvement. Even when things are going well, everything is ticking along nicely thank you very much, we are happy, the students seem happy, but then, just when we are feeling pretty comfortable with everything along comes some amazing new initiative and there goes that bandwagon driving past our classrooms and if we don't jump on, well then we are just stuck in the dark ages aren't we, we can't possibly be the great new educators of tomorrow.

Today, as teachers, we answer to so many different people and we are bombarded with emails round the clock. This phenomenon is not specific to teaching, of course. You just have to watch satirical programmes like *Utopia*, or read the increasing number of commentary and editorial pieces in the press about our modern workplaces.

But education is what I know, I have some knowledge of how schools operate in the third millennium. There are so many Deans and Directors and Deputies in schools these days, writing plans and policies and very, very important documents about what can seem like trifling issues in the greater scheme of education. We never quite know who we are supposed to be answering to and just when we think we have cleared all the administration from our desks and are sitting down to actually plan a few lessons, do some marking or write an assessment our inboxes ping giving notice of some amazing new committee that's being set up and urging us to get involved.

I'd thought that by my late-40s I'd be all grown up and in control of my destiny, moving seamlessly between work, parenting and family responsibilities but it wasn't like that at all. Like many people of my age, I am part of the sandwich generation, torn between caring for our own families while our aging parents' health begins to deteriorate. My parents back in the UK were getting old and sick. They'd come out to visit us for seven years in a row after we moved to Perth. When I left England, my dad had intimated that he wouldn't be able to make the trip over due to his many health issues, but as soon as our second son arrived they were winging their way across the world to see their newest grandson. So taken were they with this land under the sun that their pilgrimage to Perth became an annual event.

Their visits weren't without their challenges. My dad was a very stubborn man and my mum and I tended to clash, but I was happy they were able to come, and they certainly embraced the Australian way of life while they were here. Each stay had been for up to eight weeks, in the height of our summer so as to escape the grim winter months back in Britain, and I'd find a house for them to rent short term, which suited everyone. They'd hire a car and be relatively independent and it was just lovely that they were able to see our boys growing up. That made me very happy and the boys loved spending time with their English grandparents.

Being sunshine-deprived Poms they spent every possible second outdoors. No vitamin D deficiency for them. Despite my advising them the beach was best in the first part of the morning – less harmful UV rays, less wind – they tended to get to the beach around 11 am and there they would be at midday, the only people on the beach, my Dad in sandals with socks, chair turning to face the sun and quite literally frying. He had to have quite a few skin cancers removed in due course – *quelle surprise*. Our sun sense when we were growing up consisted not so much of 'slip slop slap' but of baste in that coconut oil stuff and cook. Lovely. Even in the mild climate of Northern

Ireland, where I grew up, I remember peeling layers of skin off my back and shoulders, oblivious to the harm it was doing.

Despite my alarm at my parents' lack of sun sense, and their unwillingness to take advice, we had lots of good times. Christmas around the pool was a highlight for my mum. I think my dad would have loved to live here had we emigrated earlier. They even looked at houses at one point but never quite made the mental leap that would allow them to up sticks and move hemispheres at such an advanced age.

One year Mum and Dad announced that this would be their last visit. We subsequently made the trip over to England for a couple of Christmases but increasingly the boys preferred to stay here for the summer holidays with their friends and their sporting activities under the sun. We welcomed other visitors in the meantime – one of my nephews came and stayed with us for about nine months, my niece came to stay during her honeymoon, and another nephew visited with his wife and two little boys, so we had lots of contact with the English side of the family.

Then, in 2010, tragedy struck when my eldest sister was found dead in her home at the age of 60. I found out when the phone rang in the middle of the night and my sister-in-law delivered the dreadful news. We were all devastated but it didn't come as a complete surprise. She was a troubled soul who'd sought solace in the bottle for many years; an alcoholic, in other words, something that was never fully acknowledged or accepted by my parents. I'm sure they knew but there was a lot of denial going on for a long time. I don't think my dad could ever really accept the fact that his first-born child for whom he'd had so many hopes and dreams and aspirations, his academically-brilliant daughter, who became one of the youngest consultant haematologists in the UK during the 1980s, was an alcoholic, and that her once brilliant career had ended the way it did. Dad had wanted to be a doctor himself but there wasn't the money available to fund the many years of study required. So he became a teacher and lived out his medical dreams vicariously through my sister and my brother, who is also a doctor. Dee came out to visit us with Mum and Dad on two occasions and spent most of each visit in a permanent state of inebriation. It was very difficult. I remember turning around one morning when we were all outside on the deck and watching her take an opened bottle of white wine from the fridge, pour the contents into a mug and down it in one. When I tackled Mum and Dad about her behaviour they stalled and refused to engage in a discussion, Dad telling me that she'd promised him she wasn't drinking any more and that I must have been imagining things. When she died, the official coroner's verdict was heart failure but it was pretty clear to me that she'd drunk herself to death. My brother told me later that her house was in a frightful state, with bottles everywhere. It was a squalid end to an all too short and occasionally brilliant life.

Something of a child prodigy, my sister went off to medical school in Belfast when she was 17. I was only four at the time. By 21 she was pregnant and married under a cloud of secrecy and shame. Ireland in the 1960s was not exactly a liberal, tolerant and progressive society. In my parents' eyes, and in the eyes of the community, sex before marriage was a deadly sin. During this time she managed to keep her studies going and in due course found herself working as a junior doctor in Belfast at the height of the 'troubles.' She also had some artistic talent and I have vague memories of some of her paintings. As a teenager she wrote mature and insightful articles that belied her years, and she made up stories to entertain my brother and me on long car journeys. I have always thought it such a shame she didn't pursue her creative side. It would have given her an outlet, and maybe even helped her to face and conquer her many demons. It also makes me sad beyond words that I never really knew my big sister and that she died such a tragic death.

Her shotgun marriage was a disaster and she was divorced in less than ten years, but it did produce two lovely boys, one of whom eventually headed to America. David now lives in Texas with his wife and children, to whom he is clearly devoted. I can't really comment on his relationship with my sister, that is not my story to tell, but I think that it was strained to say the least as he moved into adulthood. I haven't seen him for many many years, or met his two children, but we are now connected through Facebook. He seems really happy with his life and I would like to know him better. But the smiling faces I see on Facebook are no substitute for a real-life connection and sometimes only serve to emphasise just how far apart we are.

His brother, Peter, and I, were very close until I moved to Australia – I will never forget the joy of becoming his aunt at the age of ten – but then life got in the way. I've seen him occasionally over the years at family events and I am really glad he has a stable family life, with a lovely wife and two little boys, especially given the upheaval of his own earlier years. As a young aunt I often used to look after my two eldest nephews; I absolutely adored them and have very happy memories of when they were growing up. For a long time they felt more like my little brothers and I am sad that we are no longer close.

The weeks following my sister's death were a blur. I didn't go back for her funeral, a decision I agonised over, but in the end I stayed in Australia. While I felt it was the right decision, it was at this time I began to experience feelings of guilt and a creeping sense of anxiety. It marked the start of a very difficult period during which I felt permanently torn between my family in Australia and my family back in the UK.

When my sister died my dad was nearly 90. He was old and tired and two years later he too departed this life. They say that all families are dysfunctional in some way or another, but I find our family dynamic particularly strange. The tragedy of my sister's life and death was rarely, if ever, discussed. Being on the other side of the world and out of the loop in many ways, I can only speak for myself, but there was no sense of closure or resolution for me.

In the summer after my sister died my younger son, Ben, and I went back to England for my niece's wedding and spent some time with Mum and Dad. This was only a few months after they'd lost their first-born child, but Dee's death was barely mentioned and certainly not discussed. There was a gaping hole of silence. I agree with Marty Rubin who said that 'unexpressed grief leaves the deepest scars.' I'm pretty sure losing Dee in such tragic circumstances and in such an untimely way broke my dad's heart. He'd kept her on a pedestal for so long – his brilliant daughter who'd become the doctor he'd always wanted to be. He couldn't see the reality of the situation and believed in the fantasy daughter he'd created in his mind. The gulf between that and the reality of the situation was too much to bear, and more than he was able to face.

Mum was a little more open to talking about Dee, but never with the honesty and openness I craved. As my dad grew weaker she nursed him stoically, and as he approached the end of his life she began to talk about Dee waiting for him to join her. I think she drew comfort from the idea of my sister, cleansed of all her earthly failings, waiting for Dad in the sky.

My heart ached for my parents. Losing a child goes against the natural order of things. Having to deal with such unspeakable grief at the end of their lives, when they deserved a little peace, seemed barbaric. My mum had a very simple faith in God and in eternal life and that definitely sustained her to some extent. Throughout this time I was tormented by guilt that I couldn't be with my parents. I had responsibilities in Perth. I had my job and my own family. I sensed pressure coming from my brother and sister. The anxiety began, born of the guilt of feeling that I wasn't doing as I should, that I wasn't a good daughter, a good sister, that I was putting my husband, children and my job before my parents.

As soon as the school year ended I jumped on a plane and went to my dad's hospital bedside. He was shrivelled and dying. I stayed at my brother's house but felt uneasy about the gulf that seemed to have opened up between us in the past two years, and an even bigger one between me and my sister-in-law. It was a tense time. There was no warm, comfortable family gathering around a dying father's beside and my anxiety increased. I spent as much time as I could with Mum, going with her to see Dad in hospital each day. But I felt inadequate, slightly detached, and guilty that I was missing my family in Perth.

In the end I came home in time for Christmas. It was clear Dad wasn't going to get any better, but I wanted to be at home. When I received the inevitable phone call on New Year's Eve I spent days agonising over whether to fly back for his funeral. I'd been feeling unwell since returning home, and having been to see my GP, I took his advice not to fly back to the UK.

Two weeks later I received another phone call, this time with the dreadful news that a former colleague had taken her own life. I went back to work to start the school year, my head foggy, my mind cloudy. I couldn't see it at the time but I was unravelling. This time I went to the funeral. Numb. I held on for two more weeks and then came the day when I very publicly fell apart. I quite literally collapsed, sobbing and broken. I was done. I had nothing left to give.

Sometimes falling apart is the bravest act of all.
~ **Sarah Hackley,** ***Women Will Save the World***

Chapter 2

> *I don't want to see anyone. I lie in the bedroom with the curtains drawn and nothingness washing over me like a sluggish wave. Whatever is happening to me is my own fault. I have done something wrong, something so huge I can't even see it, something that's drowning me. I am inadequate and stupid, without worth. I might as well be dead.*
>
> ~ **Margaret Atwood**, *Cat's Eye*

It's strange but true that having depression was a good thing for me in a weird kind of way. I wouldn't wish it on my worst enemy and I wouldn't want to go through it again, but it has made me more like myself and it has made me like myself more. It has given me a much greater appreciation of all my blessings, of all that I have to be grateful for and for the beauty of the world around me. It has helped me understand and accept my innate introversion and shyness. I'm a pleaser. At school, and to some extent at university, I'd never been part of the in crowd. I wanted people to accept me, I wanted to be popular, but I never felt like I fitted in.

Now, years after that insecure girl was making poor choices and bad decisions my eyes have finally been opened to a fuller and better way of living, to a long awaited acceptance and understanding of who I really am and why none of us should never be ashamed of who we are. As my friend Sarah told me afterwards – and Sarah is a very enlightened person – what happened to me was a breakthrough rather than a breakdown, a wake-up call I needed to make some serious changes in my life.

What's wrong with you? I would say to myself, as one miserable, meaningless day merged into another. Get a grip you ungrateful, pathetic excuse for a human being. There you are in your lovely leafy western suburb with two amazing children and a wonderful, if imperfectly dressed, husband who has been completely and utterly devoted to you throughout your marriage. Toughen up, you selfish, self-obsessed, ungrateful woman, I hear as you join in with my self-admonishment. You with your array of fully matching work-out gear and your part-time work that allows you to pursue all those personal growth enhancing activities. What's wrong with you? You with your foreign travel each year and all those interests in which you have completely lost interest.

I do indeed have lots and lots of interests, ranging from my recently cultivated penchant for colouring in to musical theatre. I've always loved sport, keep relatively fit, actually quite enjoy going to the gym, I dabble in a bit of yoga and meditation, love hiking, going to the cinema, walking on the beach at sunset, swimming in the sea. And reading. I love reading. I need to read. If I haven't got a good book on the go I get really twitchy and restless. The list of my activities is endless. I'm active Sue. I'm Sue who's reasonably intelligent and pretty OK at most things she does. And I live in WA, one of the most beautiful places of the world. What the hell was wrong with me? Why couldn't I cope? But that's the point. You may well be asking yourself these questions. Believe me, I asked them of myself time and again. I felt ashamed, ungrateful and oh so very guilty, and I'm not even Catholic. On top of the depression, the guilt and shame I felt was almost unbearable. I kept telling myself that I should be able to pull myself together or click my fingers and snap out of it. But that's not how it works. I know that now but I didn't when I was right in the middle of it. Depression does not discriminate based on social standing, or race, or sex or profession. It has no rhyme or reason. It can affect anyone, even people who, on the surface, appear to have absolutely no reason to feel depressed or anxious. It doesn't matter what size your house is or what your postcode is. Filling your shopping trolley with quinoa, chia and goji berries does not make you immune to the black dog. There is no one size fits all with depression and anxiety. They are not figments of someone's imagination. They are very, very real for the sufferer. Each person experiences it differently and each person's recovery will follow a different path. All I can do is describe what is was like for me.

At my worst, I felt like there was a tsunami in my head, sweeping me along, completely out of control. My usual ability to concentrate and focus for long periods of time deserted me. I completely lost my normally sparkling sense of humour, couldn't smile or laugh and had no interest whatsoever in all the activities that give me such pleasure. Everything just seemed interminably bleak. I was incapable of completing the easiest of tasks or make the simplest of decisions, and felt totally overwhelmed by daily life.

Everything was too hard and on top of that I was stressed and confused as to why I was feeling so wretched. My brain was all fogged up and I had the very strange sensation of not really being in my body, of observing myself from afar. I was extremely irritable, didn't want to see anyone and developed an intolerance for noise and activity around me. On top of the mental trauma and the deep sense of sadness, emptiness and pointlessness, I experienced physical pain all over my body. In one particularly awful week I stopped eating and lost six kilos (would that I could do that now – on second thoughts, give me my rapidly expanding belly anytime).

I had a permanent sense of dread that bad things would happen. Despite being exhausted to the point of despair I couldn't sleep and spent night after night lying awake with my heart racing and my pulse pounding in my head. The more I couldn't sleep the more desperate I became. I withdrew completely, and there is no-one more withdrawn than a shy introvert who is depressed. I felt like an absolute failure and lost all my confidence. I kept telling myself that I should be able to cope. I was self-stigmatising and judging myself unworthy. I just wanted to push everyone away as I couldn't bear what was happening to me. Luckily, my immediate family and closest friends refused to be pushed away.

> *Do you not see how necessary a world of pains*
> *and troubles is to school an intelligence and make it a soul?*
> ~ **John Keats**, ***Letters of John Keats***

Chapter 3

In the middle of the journey of life I came to myself within a dark wood where the straight way was lost.

~ **Dante**

One of the most interesting things about my journey through anxiety and depression – from a black pit of despair and a twisted maze of turmoil to a light so bright it sometimes hurts my eyes – is that I truly believe it has made me a better person. I never thought I would find myself broken and empty in the middle of my life, a sobbing mess, hollowed out, numb, lost, consumed by the blank despair that had wrapped itself around me. I was surrounded by people who loved me but I couldn't have felt more alone. It was a huge wake-up call. It was as if this was where I needed to be for the new me to emerge.

How does that work? Something to do with there being no joy without pain, I think. The deeper the pain, the more exquisite the subsequent joy when it finally arrives. My first labour was like nothing I'd ever prepared for or could possibly have imagined in my worst nightmare. There I was with my incense, my candles, my Aztec pan-pipe music and my bean bag, only to discover that this was not going to be the blissed-out-in-tune-with-my-body drug-free deep-breathing natural birth I was so convinced would be mine.

For twenty-eight hours of agony I thought I was going to die, I thought that I would never manage to get the baby out.

And then, just as the doctors were deciding whether to transfer me to a different ward for an emergency caesarean, Daniel took it upon himself to enter this world. I think of that day, and I understand. I understand the need to suffer in order to get to something better. It may sound perverse but I absolutely believe that.

Sitting in the hospital ward the next day, looking out the window with my beautiful bundle in my arms, I felt no pain, no hurt, and I wasn't suffering any more. I had laboured and pushed and found a strength I didn't know I had, and now I was in the light with my baby in my arms experiencing a sense of joy so profound that I felt connected to the whole universe. It was transcendent and deeply, deeply spiritual. I'd lost that feeling over the years, and it took my depression to jolt me back to who I am and to discover what really matters.

Eventually and somewhat reluctantly, I saw a GP. Years of conditioning, of thinking I should be able to cope, made it feel like an admission of failure, of defeat. Looking back I see the folly in these thought patterns and realise how dangerous such a warped perception can be. It was clear I needed help, that I wasn't functioning and that I risked losing control altogether if I didn't reach out. I couldn't drive, I'd stopped eating proper meals, sleep was rare, and I cried rivers of pain and grief. The tears that started in the school quad went on for weeks and weeks. I needed to cry and wail and scream and shout and get it all out. But tears alone weren't going to fix me. Professional help was what I needed.

We have a lovely family GP in an old-fashioned surgery that doesn't even have a computer. It's like stepping back into the 50s. Old-time music on the radio, five-year-old magazines, a slightly bossy receptionist with a heart of gold, and George our lovely doctor who has cared for my boys since birth, stitching them up when necessary, administering vaccinations and tending to all the usual childhood ailments. For all practical matters, even for the dreaded Pap smears, I was quite happy to put myself in Dr George's capable hands, but when it came to my mental health he wasn't the man for me.

I found a no-nonsense female GP who set me on the road to recovery. It was she who listened to my descriptions of sleepless nights, and pounding chest, my sense of guilt and shame, my feelings of desperation and pointlessness, my suicidal thoughts. It was she who told me in no uncertain terms that I was depressed – no surprise there; highly anxious too – well knock me down with a feather. But also that it was nothing, absolutely nothing to be ashamed of. I wouldn't feel guilty if I had a broken arm, or cancer or the flu, would I?

She explained that I was experiencing a common medical condition. My brain wasn't quite working as it should, just like people's hearts, and livers and kidneys sometimes don't work as they should. I was getting help and I would get better. Of that she had no doubt. There was something about the certainty with which she spoke that broke through my desolation. I didn't fully believe her initially, but she seemed so poised and competent and in control of everything that I was slightly in awe of her and something inside me must have trusted her.

She was very young – about half my age. *Who is this crazy middle-aged woman*, she must have thought to herself. But she was efficiency personified and very clear in communicating what I needed to do to get better. As a starting point, she wanted me to take a brand of anti-depressants that was also effective at reducing anxiety. I resisted for a while, stubbornly believing that I didn't need any kind of chemical help, but in the end I gave in. It took some time for me to adjust to the prescribed medication. The doctor had warned me that I might feel worse initially – I didn't think that was possible but I found to my horror that she was right. And yet in some kind of twisted way that was also comforting.

She'd told me to expect the worst, so when it happened I thought this woman might just know a thing or two. I went through about three weeks of absolute hell. The anxiety increased and I felt like a prisoner in my head, a slave to my endless negative thoughts, my racing mind, the constant rehashing of past wrongs, hurts, betrayals and losses. Depression takes over your mind and inhabits every waking moment. It distorts the past and twists the future, making the present a living hell. There was no let up, no respite. Ever. I was disabled by self-hatred, despair, isolation, guilt and shame. One particular night I remember just clinging to my husband and shaking and crying, hour after hour. I really don't know how I got through those weeks. But I kept remembering the doctor telling me that I would get better, that I just had to go through the initial stages of adjustment before the medication would do its job. And she was right.

And yet, even when my body had stabilised I remained contracted inside myself for months, unable to share in jokes or laughter or engage fully in everyday conversation. I was paranoid about what people would think of me if they knew what was going on inside my head. My instinct was to retreat from the world and shut down all avenues of communication. As well as having to navigate through the minefield of depression and anxiety, I was extremely distressed by the detrimental effect my condition was starting to have on some of my relationships. After taking a few weeks off work, I wanted to get back into the classroom, to feel useful again, and it helped to some extent to be back at the chalk face, doing the job that I had always loved. But each day was still a battle, and how I continued to work I will never know. I was in a very dark place.

Depression isn't just being a bit sad. It's feeling nothing. It's not wanting to be alive anymore.

~ **J K Rowling**

Chapter 4

*I'm on my way,
from misery to happiness today,
ah ha ah ha ah ha ah ha.*

~ The Proclaimers

It did eventually stop. Someone heard my plea in the night and the pain began to ease, the flicker of a flame appeared in the darkness. It didn't happen suddenly, I didn't just snap out of it. There was, perhaps, a growing awareness that I was beginning to feel a bit more like my old self, or rather, like a new self, but it was a very gradual process. A turning down of the volume of the noise in my head, a hesitant lifting up of my eyes so that I could see more of what was going on around me rather than being absorbed in the hell of my mind. After a few months, I realised that I wasn't feeling quite so anxious. One day I actually smiled and joined in a conversation about something stupid in *Family Guy* or *Modern Family* or one of those shows my boys like to watch.

And then came a particular day when, even though I was still very fragile, I realised I was beginning to feel like myself again, not like some impostor, or as if an alien from outer space was inhabiting my body. On this particular day, I finally began to believe that I could and would recover from depression and learn to manage my anxiety to the extent that

I could live a full and joyful life. I had a long way to go, but I was on my way. My recovery could begin. Little did I know quite how transforming my recovery would be.

It was a strange day because I was ironing. I never iron. Somehow I'd taken pity on my husband's frantic search for a freshly-ironed shirt that morning so, finding myself with an hour on my hands after work I took the plunge. That was a revelation in itself. Realising that I had a hour in which I might be able to achieve something useful. We had a lady who came in to do our ironing for a while but one day she told us she could no longer continue as she had a problem with her knees. Her knees? Have you every heard anything so ridiculous?

Once Annie with the sore knees had abandoned us the ironing basket returned to its default overflowing position. I'm a crap ironer. Especially men's shirts. I can't be bothered with all the little pleats, the cuffs, the collars, the sleeves, and which order to do it all. I'm hopeless. If God had meant me to iron he wouldn't have invented polycotton sheets. And now with the M & S website delivering free of charge to Australia for orders over $50 there is simply no excuse for ever buying anything that needs ironing. And I'm not one of those attentive wives who always ensures her husband looks immaculate. No, not me, I have too much else to fit in what with coffee with Gaye or Jodie and my one-on-one yoga sessions with Marie; far too much to think about what with dealing with my mid-life, mental health crisis and finding my way through menopause without going completely crazy, attempting to halt the advance of my rapidly expanding stomach and pursuing my new found love for colouring in.

Anyway, on this particular day as I was gamely tackling our permanently full ironing basket while watching Phil and Kirsty weave their property magic, I knew something was different as soon as Ian walked through the door.

"Hi darling, look at me, look what I'm doing. Aren't I just the perfect middle-aged, getting through menopause without even breaking sweat, housewife?"

Silence. Nothing. No reply.

"Is everything OK? Did the photocopier break down again just when you needed to print off all those carefully scaffolded work sheets you'd prepared for your Year 11s?"

Still nothing. Something was very wrong.

"OK, well I'm here if you want to talk."

Ian left the room and I returned to my ironing, smoothing out creases like a Stepford wife as if my life depended on it. Ian is always cheerful, he is never quiet and moody, he is the least complicated person I know. That's why I love him. He's as steady as a rock. He might ride the dodgem cars or the teacups occasionally if he wants to let his salt and pepper hair down but his temperament is as even as a nil all draw. Well, most of the time. Me, I'm a little more up and down, more a rollercoaster kind of girl, but that's why we work. Yin and yang, Toshack and Keegan, The Captain and Tenille.

"Suze, first of all, you are ironing, and you hate ironing, and second of all do you realise what you have just said?" Engrossed in the task at hand I jumped as Ian came back into the room.

"Whaddya mean? Are you referring to my cheerful greeting and sparkling humour?"

"Well, yes actually. Do you realise how long it has been since you actually said something funny? It's been months Suze, months and months and months."

I stopped in my tracks, mid-crease.

Ian had come close to me now. He was gazing at me with the strangest look on his face.

"Are you feeling OK Sue, have you been drinking?"

"Oh that's charming. Thanks, darling. Of course I haven't been bloody well drinking. It's four in the afternoon. I never have a drink until at least 4.15."

"There you go again, sweetie. You're being funny – well, you're attempting to be funny."

"Thanks very much, Ian. Lovely to have my witty repartee torn to shreds. Love you too, honey."

"And you look different. You look … lighter somehow."

Hang on. He was right. Oh my God. He was right. It had been months and months and months. Months of crippling, frightening, debilitating depression and gut-wrenching anxiety, followed by several more months of feeling marginally better but still nowhere like myself. Months of doing my best to get through each day but feeling somehow numbed from reality and detached from my life, as if I were floating above myself somewhere, observing but not really participating in everything going on around me. Going through the motions, existing rather than living, here but not here, checked out. But here I was today, ironing without a care in the world, joining in with Phil and Kirsty's banter, and, oh my goodness, had I actually been humming?

I put down the iron, not noticing that I had placed it right in the middle of Ian's best white shirt.

"Sue, did something happen today to put you in a good mood?"

"No, not really." I wrinkled my nose and thought for a moment. Then, "OH MY GOD, do you think I might just be getting better?" I said tentatively, as realisation dawned. And then a more confident, cautiously excited, "I think I may just possibly be on my way back."

"Sue, let's just stay calm about this, let's not get carried away just yet."

"Calm is not the word that springs to mind when one realises that one may just possibly, just very possibly, be approaching the light at the end of a very deep dark and long tunnel," said I, my hope mounting by the second.

"Why are you talking like the Queen?"

"I'm not talking like the Queen, and she would never say that because she would never get depressed due to her general wonderfulness." There it is again, my slight obsession with the Royal Family.

"Right, that's three quips. You're definitely on your way back Sue."

He had tears in his eyes. I looked at my lovely, patient, kind and long-suffering husband and saw all the pain of the world on his face. I saw the pain and anguish of our annus horribilis – see, told you I loved the Queen – but there amongst it I saw hope. Hope that he might just be getting his wife back. Hope that this nightmare might be over. I suddenly realised this wasn't just about me. It was about all of us. He had been there with me every step of the way. He had held me all night while I shook and sobbed. He had kept the household running when I couldn't get out of bed. He had tried to keep his spirits up and jolly everyone along when I was blank, listless and despondent.

I looked down as smoke rose from the ironing board accompanied by the acrid smell of burning, and I lifted the steaming iron to reveal a dark brown imprint on Ian's best white shirt. We looked at each other and then we just started laughing. Laughing and crying and hugging as if our lives depended on it.

"Oh well, housework was never my forte," I said. One ruined Pierre Cardin shirt was a small price to pay for this magical moment when I finally believed that I was going to be OK.

There is a light that never goes out.
~ **The Smiths**

Chapter 5

I only went out for a walk and finally concluded to stay out till sundown, for going out, I found, was really going in.
~ **John Muir,** ***John of the Mountains: The Unpublished Journals of John Muir***

That was three years ago. That was the moment I realised I had managed to change my lightbulb. You know those jokes. I made up my own.

How many people with depression does it take to change a lightbulb?

None – it won't happen. There is no point changing the light bulb. The world will still be bleak and black. And anyway, no-one has the energy or can be bothered to change it.

How many people with anxiety does it take to change a lightbulb?

An infinite number. One to have a panic attack about the responsibility of having to do it, one to worry endlessly about which type of light bulb to use – the choice is overwhelming; one to worry pointlessly about whether the right decision has been made; one to worry about the possibility of getting electrocuted; one to worry in case the globe is faulty and doesn't work; one to be anxious about the chance that it might fuse and affect all the other electrical appliances in the house; one to worry about what other people will think of the new lightbulb and one to be very very afraid of being judged.

That was me for a while. Both those scenarios described me exactly. But with patience and persistence and no small amount of determination, I was able to recover. I changed my lightbulb and now I'm pretty sure I can change lightbulbs all by myself. If you are in that dark place now, you can too. You can and will change your lightbulb. Just hold on. In the words of that great songsmith, Michael Stipe, just hold on, don't let go, don't ever let go. There is always hope. I nearly gave up hope. I was on the verge of packing it all in, giving up, signing out forever from this mortal coil. But I didn't. The light came back on. And yours will too. You have to believe that.

When we had untangled ourselves from our laughing, crying and hugging, Ian had to run off to a meeting – he's always running off to meetings. If he was paid pro-rata for the amount of hours he spends in meetings and talking to parents, we wouldn't be agonising over every dollar we need to spend on our house renovation, or whether we can afford to have semi-commercial window frames instead of the bog-standard frames from the builder's standard range. Sunergy glazing or Comfort Plus, sliders, stackers or bi-folds? So many decisions, so much money. But I digress. I packed away the ironing board and iron and disposed of the ruined shirt as I attempted to process how I was actually feeling and what had just happened.

Now, gradually, despite the trials of menopause, a mid-life crisis, an expanding waistline, and one completely ruined Pierre Cardin shirt, was the light finally creeping back into my life? Hearing the front door close behind Ian I went to the bedroom and quickly changed into my favourite leggings, coordinating hoody and my blue and pink trainers, plugged myself into my new rose-gold iphone complete with my lovingly created Spotify playlist with a beat that perfectly matched my stride and headed out the door.

That's what I do. I walk. When I need to clear my head I walk. I love the fresh air, the blue sky, the trees, the beauty all around me. I love feeling the pavement beneath my feet, the rhythmic beat, words and melodies in my ears. My mind clears, my breath steadies, ideas come to me, solutions to problems somehow magically appear. Over the last year, though, I'd been walking with my head down and my mind clogged with endless rehashing of the past, fear about the future, walking robotically to numb the pain and the debilitating pointlessness that engulfed me. For a very scary few months there had even been times when I didn't want to keep going, when I thought there was about as much chance of England ever again making it to the final of the football World Cup as there was of me feeling anything remotely like my old self ever again.

But here I was, striding along, greeting fellow walkers and the occasional jogger, casting my eye all around and just marvelling at the wonderful ordinariness of my leafy suburb. So maybe 2018 will be England's year, and like a phoenix the three lions will rise from the ashes (something not quite right there with the phoenix and the lions, but whatever) of their European disgrace. Actually that would be great – we could plan a trip to Russia. Well maybe not, I don't really fancy Russia, what with all those doping scandals and that dreadful Putin person. Knowing my luck I'd be thrown in jail for criticising the government like I once criticised the managing director of a company I worked for prior to becoming a teacher and never see my family again. Well I didn't never see my family again because I criticised the managing director, but

I did end up resigning from that job. Slightly different from being thrown in a Russian jail but still fairly traumatic at the time. Maybe Qatar in 2022. The airline is pretty good, there's a direct flight from Perth and we could pop over to see Simon and Daria in Dubai afterwards.

I digress again. Let me tell you a bit more about myself.

As you already know I am married to the frequent-meeting attendee, Ian, who like me is a teacher, but who unlike me is calm, rational and even-tempered, apart from those rare occasions in his life when he has attempted to wield an Allen key to assemble flat-pack furniture. We have two boys. Daniel is twenty and currently travelling around Europe, after a semester's exchange in Lyon. Right now he is probably in a bar near the Plaza Mayor, thought I as Sia began swinging from the chandelier, sipping a caña or a cuba libre; or he'd be strumming his guitar on a beach or in a youth hostel somewhere, lost in the wonder of being young and free.

Before Daniel left for his European exchange I'd given him all the talks I thought any responsible parent should give a child when they set off on their first big adventure. Daniel had travelled a lot before. He'd done a month's exchange while he was in Year 11, staying with the most wonderful family in a little village near Fontainebleau, about an hour south of Paris. He's a lucky boy; they adore him and vice versa and have provided him with a second home ever since. There are five children in the family and a blind St Bernard called Maggie, and they live in a big old three-storey house with a walled garden. It is very reassuring knowing that he can go there anytime he likes while he's in Europe. He left most of his stuff there when he went off travelling. The dad, Olivier, plays in a band and Dan thinks he is just the coolest guy ever and loves jamming with him. In fact, I'm pretty sure it was Olivier who inspired him to start learning to play the guitar properly, the one I bought him when he was fourteen, the one that sat in his wardrobe for three years in the days before Ed Sheeran burst onto the scene and Daniel realised that it was acceptably cool to play the acoustic guitar.

So anyway, despite being a seasoned traveller and having received all the appropriate health and sex education at school, I always give Dan a refresher course before he travels. "Yes Mum, sure Mum," he says, nodding a lot and looking just a little bit embarrassed. He thinks I talk about sex far too much. "Why do you always have to bring up sex, Mum?" he says, "why do you always pick up on innuendo and double entendres, Mum?"

Because it's funny, and it's important to be able to talk about these things. I must be overcompensating for the lack of information and communication on the subject from my own parents. Such was their inability to prepare the four of us for the big wide world that when my eldest sister went off to university she was pregnant within a couple of years. And she was studying medicine for God's sake. And they still didn't talk about it. In fact I didn't find out until I was a lot older – I was ten at the time. It was all cloak and dagger and suffocating silence and shame and just don't talk about stuff or say anything that might possibly upset someone.

I don't really get that thing people say about parents doing their best because that was all they knew. If I followed my parents' example I would be the same but I'm pretty sure my parenting style is about as different as you could possibly get. I love that my boys talk to me about pretty much anything. I love that they were happy for me to come with them to the Ed Sheeran concert, even if they were shifting rather uncomfortably in their seats while I was dancing and cheering and screaming for more and waving my arms in the air.

Daniel's brother Ben is three years younger and they are polar opposites. But they adore each other. Possibly because their personalities are so different, even though they share similar interests. We never experienced any of the rivalry, one-up-personship and general mistrust that can be so prevalent amongst siblings. On the day Ben was born three-year-old Daniel could barely contain his excitement, appearing by my bedside in the birthing centre with his favourite teddy bear, Snowy, his gift for his baby brother. My own brother cried on the day I was born as he wanted a little brother so badly, and to this day I am convinced that he has not forgiven me for being a girl. Rumour has it that he climbed up on my pram one day and I catapulted out, landing on my head. That explains a lot, or so I am told. Both my older sisters told me at varying times that they hated me when I was a teenager and young adult, not an unusual thing for siblings to say to each other, but in a sensitive soul such as mine it created scars for life. Family baggage. Don't you just love it?

Back to my own marvellous children. Daniel is a dreamer, a feeler, a deep thinker. Ben is a doer. Daniel moves through life on Daniel time, while Ben times everything to precision and hates being late. Both are talented sportsmen but while Ben is a fierce competitor, Daniel lacks the same competitive drive. But he is supremely fit, works out nearly every day and loves running for the sheer pleasure of it. He didn't get that from me. I hate running – too many bits that jangle up and down for my liking. And now with the expanding stomach, far too uncomfortable. No, it's walking for me thank you very much.

You ask Ben to do the washing up and it will be done in double quick time so that he can get on to the next thing. Dan on the other hand, has been known to spend more than five minutes drying one plate while he gazes into the distance, pondering the meaning of life or chuckling to himself as he relives something he heard or saw, or cites extracts from his favourite films or Monty Python skits. As in life, so in birth. Daniel took a total of twenty-eight hours deciding whether or not to come out of my cosy womb into the big wide world; Ben whooshed out in three hours before I had a chance to utter the words: "get me the bloody Pethidine."

Both boys miraculously skipped that monosyllabic adolescent phase that other parents warned me about. It never happened. Or maybe they are late developers. I have many faults but I think I am a good mother and I am proud of how I have brought my boys up and the fine young men they are becoming. I adore them, they are my world and the best thing I ever did, and I'm pretty sure they think I am OK too. Despite my penchant for embarrassing them in shops and restaurants and public places in general, complaining about poor service, or jumping the queue at airports, or talking to their friends using expressions like 'whateves' and 'catcha,' (no-one says that anymore Mum) or posting photos of them on Facebook with captions expressing my pride and joy at their very existence and myriad achievements.

We are a close knit bunch and do lots and lots of things together as a family, and lots and lots of talking. There wasn't a lot of talking when I was growing up. There was a lot of: "go to your room, Susan, and finish your Latin translation before you watch any television;" or, "89% in your English Literature examination is a bit disappointing, Susan;" or, "no, you can't go to that party all your friends are going to Susan, this is an important year and you need to focus on getting the best A level results you can."

There was a lot of that kind of talking but very little two-way, I am really listening to you and your opinion and feelings do matter kind of talking. In our family, my boys are the sensible ones and I am the irresponsible one. They say things like, "do you really need that third glass of wine, Mum?" or, "you seemed a bit pissed when you were singing Karaoke tonight, Mum." They look out for me. They've had nothing to rebel against and consequently are two of the most (touch wood) well-adjusted, open, communicative, kind, friendly and compassionate people I know. Oh my God Sue, I hear you say, get over yourself, so you think your kids are amazing, we all do, enough already. But I make no apology. My children are truly amazing.

As Years and Years declared that nothing could hurt them with their eyes shut, I squeezed mine tightly shut to see if anything hurt, to make sure I hadn't imagined my newfound sense of well-being. I squeezed some more and kept walking, my right foot gave way, I wobbled and fell, landing painfully on the side of my right buttock. I opened my eyes, wiggled my nose – dog poo. How absolutely undignified. But do you know what, I didn't care. I didn't care that I could smell the poo and my backside was throbbing. I threw back my head and started to laugh rather maniacally, drawing strange looks from passing dog walkers in the park across the road. I laughed and then I started to cry. I started sobbing with the sheer relief of being able to feel something other than absolute despair.

Light existed all along. Of course it did.
Who says it didn't because I couldn't see it?

~ **Gillian Marchenko**

Chapter 6

Heaven knows we need never be ashamed of our tears, for they are rain upon the blinding dust of earth, overlying our hard hearts. I was better after I had cried, than before — more sorry, more aware of my own ingratitude, more gentle.

~ Charles Dickens

    Like Jude (swoon) Law's character in *The Holiday* I am a big weeper. I cry when I'm sad, I cry when I'm happy. I cry if my boys score a goal or a half century. A beautiful piece of music, a sad or even a happy song can move me to tears. I cried during the opening sequence of *The Notebook* when the geese are flying across the lake in the sunset and I didn't stop until the closing credits. On a plane to France with a school group a few years ago my colleague and I looked up from our screens and saw tears streaming down both our faces; she was watching *Finding Neverland* while the source of my emotion was *Finding Nemo*. I love watching movies on planes. There is something cleansing and cathartic about crying while suspended in mid-air, and as you can see any film will do the trick. It's as if time stops for a while and you can just let go and let your feelings flow.

    After a while sitting on the pavement in dog poo, my sobbing eased and I looked up. The light was fading and the clouds were tinged with pink and orange as the day drew to a close. It was a glorious sight. I inhaled deeply and sighed with pleasure. My profuse weeping had released all of the tension in my body. People don't cry enough in my view. I've spent most of my life being told not to cry, telling myself to keep it together, aware of other people's awkwardness when confronted with such raw emotion. We are afraid of tears. People seem to think they are a sign of weakness. On the contrary. Crying is the body's natural response to stress and we should do much more of it.

About ten years ago we had the most wonderful time when my brother and his wife visited over Christmas and New Year. Ben was six, old enough to really understand the concept of distance and to realise that we lived a very very long way from my side of the family. On the day our visitors left, my youngest son collapsed in grief. He howled, he wailed, he rolled around on the floor in an intense and raw display of emotion for about five minutes. He had loved getting to know his uncle and aunt and it had been a very special time. Aunty Leigh had played games and read to him, and Uncle Tim had played backyard cricket with him, taken him to the park, even put his new basketball hoop together on Boxing Day, in thirty six degree heat. I was so grateful because if Ian ever has cause to open his toolkit you can be sure that within less than a minute a tirade of expletives will be issuing from his mouth. My husband has many fine qualities but DIY is not his strength.

Anyway, in Ben's eyes Uncle Tim and Aunty Leigh were the business. The best uncle and aunt you could ever wish to have. He knew it was over and he knew that it would be quite some time before we saw them again. Our visitors had brought a little of the magic of a British Christmas into our home for a few weeks.

Being an escapee from a less sunnier clime I love Christmas in Perth – beach in the morning, sumptuous seafood barbecue, drinks around the pool. We kept the same rituals that I'd inherited from my parents – they did Christmas well – stockings opened in the morning, but no tree presents until we've been to the beach, and then everyone sits round, drink in hand while the tree presents are handed out and opened one by one. It's not better or worse than Christmas in Britain. It's just different and I've embraced it. But that year, I felt a deep sense of nostalgia for my childhood Christmases and being with my brother was special. We got on better than we ever had before as adults, and I'd even felt that he might love me just a little.

Ben's reaction to their departure was pure emotion, a visceral response that he wouldn't have been able to put into words. He clung to my legs and I stroked his head as he let it all out. I didn't tell him not to cry, I didn't tell him not to be sad, I let him sob it all out. And then it was done. After about five minutes he stopped quite abruptly, stood up and trotted off to find Buzz Lightyear or Woody or Mr Potato Head. Within an hour he was back to his usual self. He was all cried out and the tears had done their job.

As adults we rarely do that. We've long lost that childhood capacity to express ourselves. We keep it together, we cry a little maybe but hold back from really letting rip with our tears, our feelings, our emotions, our grief. Trouble is, each time we withhold something, those feelings remain. With nowhere to go they fester, somewhere deep down inside perhaps but they are there. Something else happens, we suffer a wrong, a hurt, another loss, we don't fully explore the depth and breadth of our reactions, we put our lipstick on and carry on with the busyness of our lives, with all our obligations and responsibilities and stuff we simply have to do. We keep up appearances, we stay silent for fear of offending people. Each time we face a trauma or a crisis or a loss and don't fully purge our grief, it stays there, it stagnates until eventually all that unexpressed emotion and sadnesses implodes, often with disastrous consequences.

At least that's what happened to me. I can't speak for anyone else but that is how is was for little old me. I wish that as an adult I could be more like Roald Dahl's *Matilda* and put things right as I go along, stand up for myself more. Thank you, Tim Minchin, by the way for your musical and lyrical genius in composing one of the best musicals I've ever seen. Who'd have thought I'd be so moved by a musical about a little girl. It was spectacular, uplifting, hilarious and deeply deeply moving all at once. During those three hours in the Princess Theatre in Melbourne I was truly transported. That is what all great art and entertainment should do in my view. Take us somewhere else for a while and make us feel that anything is possible, that we can change the world if we put our minds to it, that there is always the hope of a brighter day, that wrongs can be righted and records set straight. So thank you Tim Minchin. I can't wait to see your version of Groundhog Day, which is one of my favourite films. The next time you are in Perth could you please come round to dinner. We all just love you in our household. We love that graduation speech you gave at UWA, and we loved watching you as Judas in Jesus Christ Superstar at Perth Arena. We love what you did for the victims of abuse by the Catholic Church. We think you are one awesome human being.

Enough of this idolatry.

I stood up carefully, took off my shoe and wiped off as much of the dog poo as I could on the grass verge. I looked around. The remaining dog walkers were heading home from the park opposite. I crossed the street and sat on a bench, gazing at the trees swaying in the breeze and the dappled sky and I thought. I thought for a long time as the sun sank behind the horizon and the sky darkened. I thought about all that I had been through in the last few years. I thought and I thought. As you can probably tell I am a huge over-thinker. My parents always seemed uncomfortable with this tendency of mine. "Why do you always have to tell us what you're thinking?" they would say. "Don't think about it, Susie." As if stopping thinking about it would have stopped the bullying or the teasing, or would stop my best friend when I was fourteen from dumping me for Marion Johnson and breaking my heart, or stop the children in Africa from starving or stop the senseless slaughter of baby seals.

It was OK to think about stuff like differentiation and glacial erosion and the causes of the Second World War but to think about emotions and, God forbid, express them, well that just wouldn't do at all and we wouldn't want to have a 'scene' would we? I learnt to shut up and keep my thoughts to myself but I never stopped thinking them.

Now, sitting alone in the twilight, I thought and I thought and I prayed to a God I'm not sure I believe in. I prayed that I wouldn't fall back into the debilitating depression that had struck me down. I prayed that Ian and I would now be able to really embrace and enjoy our middle age and grow happily and comfortably old together. For a while there I wasn't sure. I really felt that he would be better off without me. I'd really given the sickness and worse parts of our marriage vows a bloody good work out. I wouldn't have blamed him if he decided not to stick around. I'd had a pretty checkered relationship history prior to meeting my lovely Ian.

Maybe my past was catching up with me, I would think. A happy marriage was perhaps just too good to be true. Twenty-plus years was a pretty good run in anyone's book. Maybe that would be all I would get and I would go back to being Sue who always picks the wrong guy, the bad guy, who doesn't deserve a truly good kind man like Ian. Such had been some of my rambling thoughts about our relationship while I tried to fight off my black dog. Time, maybe to call it quits. Time to release Ian from the responsibility of looking after me and putting up with my inky-black mind.

I underestimated him hugely. Ian loved me to the moon and back. He never stopped loving me. As I sat on that bench it hit me with a blinding clarity. How could I possibly have doubted him, doubted us. That's what depression and anxiety do to you. They cloud your judgement, make you lose all sense of perspective and even make you a little bit paranoid. I'd also lost all my confidence in myself. I've never been a very confident person and like the majority of women have always had some body issues. But I do realise that I'm not too bad looking and I scrub up pretty well if I say so myself. Prior to the rapidly expanding waistline I had a pretty shapely figure and I have really good hair.

Ian is not the most romantic of men. In fact, he thinks the whole idea of romance is a complete con and the main reason why people break up is because they are looking for that romantic hit again and keep seeking the high you get at the start of a relationship. He's got that just about right but there have been times when I've resented his lack of romantic gestures and could have really used the odd cheesy compliment about my appearance, voluptuous figure or spectacular taste in clothes. I like a bit of flattery now and again and I'm not averse to a little gentle flirting.

I've had my admirers over the years. There was that time when I'd gone to Tuscany for a week on my own after one of my French tours. I am sure that had I been more responsive and willing, Antonio, the charismatic wine tour guide, would have jumped at the chance to sample the delight of my curves. "Suzannnna," he would say in treacly smooth tones, "I can't believe your husband allows you to travel on your own. I wouldn't let you out of my sight," or, "Suzannnna, you are an amazing woman, your husband is a lucky man;" or, "Suzannnna, try this glass of Ruffino, it's better that having an orgasm" – yes, he really said that. He must have been crap in bed. "Suzannna, come round to my house tomorrow and I'll cook you a lasagna that will blow your mind."

You get the picture. Or how about that carpenter who built a deck for us when we first moved to Perth. I'm sure he had the hots for me. He used to pop in unannounced during the day for a while, ostensibly to hammer in a few more nails, add an extra coat of sealant or check that there'd been no warping or splitting, when I really knew that he just wanted to gaze at my beauty just one more time. A woman can sense these things.

But who would want me now, I often thought, me with my rapidly expanding midriff. People tell me I don't look my age but I've become very conscious of these two lines between my eyebrows and a crease at the top of my nose that has appeared recently. If I lift up my eyebrows they disappear but with my normal resting face they are right there and I hate them. Yes,

I'll admit it, I'm far too vain. I can hear the distant call of the Botox needle. Maybe it is time for me to check in for a little treatment. Everyone is doing it.

When my boys were at primary school one of the dads was a plastic surgeon. I could look him up. I am sure he would be only too pleased to get his hands on my crinkles and wrinkles. Years ago, on the day before a parent function I'd been hit right between the eyes with a hockey ball, just above the bridge of my nose, in fact right where that horrible little crease is, the impact creating two perfectly symmetrical and very impressive black eyes. Said plastic surgeon approached me looking hurt. "Sue darling, you've had work done and you didn't come to me." Oh yes, I could just see the dollar signs in his eyes as he scrutinised my features.

Getting back to my checkered relationship history. My parents had a really weird attitude to sex and relationships. I'm pretty sure they were each other's one and only and expected their four children to follow suit. Sex before marriage was the ultimate taboo. They clearly had a sex life themselves, they had four children for God's sake. I remember one day when I was baking with my mother – some of my happiest memories of my mum are the Saturday afternoons spent baking, the warm and homely aroma of scones and biscuits and cakes filling our modest kitchen.

On this particular day I put my hand into the pocket of the apron I was wearing and felt a strange kind of square packet. It was small and kind of squishy. A condom. At the time I had no idea what it was. I remember pulling it out and showing my mum and asking her innocently what it was. She snatched it off me, and I remember not being able to work out what the source of her discomfort was. Blimey, I thought later, when

I finally realised what a condom packet looked like, were my mother and father splayed across the kitchen table bonking away at every opportunity when we were out at scouts or hockey or youth club? It doesn't bear thinking about really. No child really wants to imagine their parents having sex. But a bit of education would have been nice, a bit of acceptance that it was part of life and yes, while it might be a bit embarrassing to talk about it, it was all perfectly normal and they clearly had as many urges as the next couple.

I had a couple of boyfriends while I was still at school that my father barely tolerated but he didn't stop me seeing them. I think he was wary after what happened with my sister and was trying to be a bit more lenient with me. That was one of the reasons my sisters said they hated me, I think. In their eyes I had a lot more freedom as a teenager than they ever had and they really resented it. I did have more freedom but nowhere near as much as my peers, and it's not my fault I was born last. By the time I was a teenager my siblings all had their own lives – both my sisters were working in England and my brother was in medical school. To a large extent I felt like an only child throughout my adolescence – I am closest in age to my brother and he is six years older than me. We never had a lot of money but there was more money for things like holidays in France and trips across to London when I was growing up. Hence my siblings' very apparent resentment about the freedom they perceived me to have.

But compared to my peers, I felt very restricted as a teenager. My dad would wait up for me to come home if I'd been out and expect me to present myself in the living room to satisfy him that I wasn't coming home blind drunk. "Have you been drinking, Susan?" he'd say. "No Dad," I would lie, even though I'd probably had about three martinis or cinzanos with lemonade. Remember those? No-one drinks those any more. Or at least no-one under the age of eighty.

And what about sherry? My parents weren't drinkers but on special occasions out would come the Waterford crystal and the Amontillado my mum drank and that really sickly sweet cream sherry stuff that my dad loved. It tasted gross but for some reason I always had some – it was the one drink my parents allowed me to consume under their roof. Probably thought it was safe given that it was a kind of old-lady drink.

I never really got drunk in those days, just a little bit merry after my three martinis or cinzanos. I wouldn't have dared – the wrath of my father would have been too much to bear. That all changed later when I left home and headed across the Irish Sea to university in England, where drinking represented freedom, escape and a whole new life. It also became a way of fitting in, feeling more confident and simply letting loose after years of feeling pretty damn repressed.

My dad always called me Susan when he was being serious or expressing his disapproval, which was pretty often throughout my teenage years. Consequently I came to really dislike my name. When I was younger my parents called me Susie most of the time. Susie was a good girl and did as she was told. Susan needed disciplining and needed to be more responsible. I was so confused about whether I was Susie the good girl, or Susan the disappointing daughter that when I went to university I decided that I would henceforth be called Sue. Now, years later, I really like the name Susan. It has a certain dignity and gravitas that pleases me these days, but it is rarely used.

In my late adolescence I had a couple of relationship break-ups that really rocked my confidence. The first time

I experienced the heartache that only a teenager can feel, I took to my bed for about a week. My parents were clearly really worried about me but do you think they would actually encourage me to talk about it? No, that would be far too obvious a thing to do. It would have be nice if they had built me up a bit, massaged my bruised ego, boosted my battered self-esteem in some way. Looking back now, I think I went into some kind of mini-depression after that first unceremonious dumping. It was certainly a fairly extreme reaction to a fairly common teenage occurrence.

A few years after that I had another crisis after another relationship ended. I found it really hard to get out of bed and get myself to lectures, and after my best friend called home my dad flew over to see me and took me back to Ireland. I remember sitting on the plane with him on the way back to Ireland and feeling his disappointment in me just seeping out of his pores. Back in the bosom of my emotionally-repressed family, there was no indication that I should perhaps see a doctor or a psychologist or at the very least talk to my parents about it. I just stayed in bed for the best part of three weeks, and then somehow emerged from what I now know must have been another depressive episode. Again, no discussion.

I came out of my adolescent reminiscing, banished the grotesque images of my parents copulating on the kitchen table, and realised that it was completely dark. I headed home. I was tired and needed to sleep. It had been a glorious day but I was quite drained. I walked home slowly, enjoying the cooler air on my face as the half moon rose in the sky. *It is all going to be OK, it is OK and it will continue to be OK*, I thought. One of my father's favourite sayings was: "This too shall pass." He never talked about the thing it was that would pass, never engaged in discussion about it, but I think it brought him comfort in a crisis to say that it would pass.

When I'd been in the pit of depression I often repeated this mantra to myself. Now I could see that it was right. It had passed. If not completely, it was well on the way to passing. It was time to begin again, to start over. I couldn't wait for tomorrow, I didn't want to waste any more time. I picked up my pace and walked back home.

To feel intensely is not a symptom of weakness, it is the trademark of the truly alive and compassionate. It is not the empath who is broken, it is society that has become dysfunctional and emotionally disabled. There is no shame in expressing your authentic feelings.
~ **Anthon St. Maarten**

Chapter 7

I love being married. It's so great to find that one special person you want to annoy for the rest of your life.
                                              ~ **Rita Rudner**

My phone beeped.

"Are you Ok?" A text from Ian.

"Yes, I'm OK. I'm still here. I haven't packed my bags and set off to find myself by walking across Mongolia." Now there's a thought. Maybe that's what I needed. Some time away to get some perspective. I'd always fancied a Joanna Lumley type adventure. Might have a bit of trouble funding it, and I don't like the idea of a camera crew following me around. And how does she always manage to look so bloody glamorous, even when drinking camel's milk and eating dates in the Sahara desert with those nomadic tribesmen she's so fond of?

"Ha ha. Want to go out for dinner tonight?"

"Sure, I'm heading home now."

"Suze, I love you."

He loved me. I know he did. He really did. Before I began to emerge from the darkness I was convinced he couldn't possibly love me anymore, especially after what I'd put him through. This is a common thought-pattern for people going through depression. In my shame and sense of worthlessness

I couldn't imagine how anyone could possibly love me or want to stay with me. But Ian and I had been through so much together, and while I didn't realise it when I was trapped in a silent nightmare, he never stopped believing that I would recover and he was with me every step of way.

In the words of WH Auden, he was my north, my south, my east, my west. Something popped into my mind, a memory of us going to watch *Ghost* early on in our relationship. You know the film, Demi Moore and Patrick Swayze getting hot and sweaty at the potter's wheel. Ian isn't super romantic. He isn't a Valentine's Day, hearts and flowers and chocolates kind of guy. But we'd enjoyed that film, we were moved by it. We rarely go to the cinema now. Ian often fidgets in his chair if he doesn't like a film, and makes it very obvious that he's not impressed, while I weep quietly but oh so sweetly as Andrew Lincoln conveys his undying love for Keira Knightley, or Jack Black finally realises he loves Kate Winslet. It's not a relaxing combination.

But I remembered watching *Ghost* just when we were beginning to realise that we might have something very special together. I thought about today's breakthrough and realised how very lucky I was to have Ian in my life. Life was too short, too precious and far too fragile not to make the very most of every remaining moment. Gosh, Sue, I think you might finally be growing up at the ripe old age of fifty-four.

I turned to my phone and typed, "Ditto."

Ian was waiting for me a little anxiously as I walked through the door.

"Sue, are you OK? I've been worried."

"Oh, I'm so sorry darling," I said. "I've just been walking. I needed some air and some space. It's not every day you realise that you are not going to be totally consumed by the blackest of dogs. Oh yes, and setting up my Tinder account if you must know. Found a very interesting chap called Sven and we're meeting tomorrow at his house."

"Ha bloody ha Sue. I was really worried about you. Don't bother about Sven. Swedes are overestimated. I'm here, anytime you want, just say the word and I'm yours," said my looking-in pretty-good-shape husband despite his penchant for crocs and complete lack of interest in fashion.

Ian and I were both very aware that our sex life had dwindled in the last few years. Now that I was feeling better I was hoping we would get back on track, and if not go at it like rabbits every night, at least have some kind of regular activity occurring in the marital bed, or anywhere else for that matter.

We used to be quite adventurous once upon a time. After my meltdown I'd lost all interest. My libido came back for a while but then menopause set in big time and what with hot flushes, mood swings, and generally feeling like crap, sex was the last thing on my mind. I was so underprepared for menopause. My mother had told me absolutely nothing about it, just like she never talked to me about sex, or childbirth. You know, important life altering events like that – never discussed in our household.

When I was about twelve I was given a big packet of those voluminous Dr White's sanitary pads, the ones with the belt and hooks, without explanation, and a little green book to read. That was the extent of the parental sexual education I received. School wasn't much better. I remember watching some programme about reproduction in Biology one day and that was it. We were left to our hormonally, emotionally charged selves to find out about the most important part of life – the reason why we are all here and the species continues to survive despite our capacity for the destruction of both the planet and our fellow humans.

Ian was always so understanding about my diminishing libido. Patient and kind and caring and understanding. But what if he was getting his rocks off else where? What if he was a liar and he was really a serial philanderer who had somehow managed to pull the wool over my eyes for years. Maybe he'd been secretly liaising with Sonia from accounts or Maria from the geography department. Oh Sue, get a grip.

"Oh darling, that's a lovely thought but I'm tired, I've got about as much energy as a person who's got no energy (similes have never been my strength – or do I mean metaphors?) and I really really need to sleep."

I hadn't been sleeping well. Another lovely side effect many women suffer when going through 'the change' as my mother used to call it, on top of which insomnia is one of the most insidious and debilitating signs of depression. As I said before, she never talked about what that mysterious change involved. I used to wonder if I would morph into some kind of Dr Who monster, or a werewolf perhaps. Quite frankly, that would be preferable to the crisis of identity and loss of confidence I suffered. In an already not-very-confident person like me it was a disaster. And the sleepless nights, tossing and turning, really ground me down.

Ian and I have very different nocturnal habits these days and I am particular about the conditions I need to have to get a good night's sleep. Long gone were the days when we'd be sandwiched together in my single bed at the beginning of our relationship, snoozing blissfully in each other's arms. These days, I like to watch TV in bed, or read and keep the light on while I drift off whereas Ian likes to listen to podcasts. He hates the light on and I get really agitated and twitchy when he's fiddling with his phone under the covers.

"No blue light in the bedroom, Ian," I snap. "It's the worst thing you can do when you are trying to get to sleep, darling."

"But you've got your bedside light on," he quips.

"It's not the same. It's a different sort of light."

Insomnia. Yet another lovely symptom of my stage of life. And even if I manage to get to sleep, the slightest thing wakes me up, such as Ian's intermittent throat clearing, or periodic snoring, the sound of which seems magnified in the dead of night. So on my worst nights when I've read as much as I can of the latest JoJo Moyes novel, done my special yogic breathing, counted backwards, forwards, recited whole passages of The Tempest in my head (rote learning chunks from the classics at school, it sets you up for life) and I am still staring at the ceiling, I pick up my pillow and go off to the spare room where I can at least toss and turn and read more JoJo if I want to without worrying about waking Ian.

I always feel guilty leaving my rightful spot in the marital bed but what's the big deal with always having to sleep together? I much prefer a little afternoon delight. We used to be really good at fitting it in during the day when the boys were younger. Now they are big hairy teenagers with raging hormones they would know exactly what Mum and Dad were doing if we said we were going to have a little rest without being able to rely on Disney Pixar to keep them entertained. Much more difficult finding the time these days. If a little window of opportunity does happen to arise at say 3 o'clock on a Saturday when Ben is out umpiring hockey and Daniel is in his room lost in his songwriting zone I am usually far too tired to rise to the occasion. Not so Ian. He can always rise to the occasion. All I have to do is say the word and he's fully risen and ready and oh so very willing. It's just so unfair.

So on more than one occasion in the last year I'd gone off to the spare room in desperation for some shut eye. I'd even been wondering for a while if it wouldn't be better all round if we had our own rooms. Then I wouldn't feel guilty about all my tossing and turning, and putting the light on to try and stave off the endless churning of my mind by attempting to read a book.

Ian hates it when I'm not there beside him but he's not missing out on any red hot sex and he's got his Radio 4 science podcasts to keep him company should he happen to stir. All that talk about protons and neutrons has him back in the land of nod in no time. Me, I don't care who is beside me or not beside me. All I care about is getting seven or eight hours of restful, interrupted sleep. But being good old dutiful Sue not wanting to upset anyone, I stick with the marital bed and keep the spare room as a somehow slightly shameful middle of the night option when I can't stand being awake for one more minute.

On top of our opposing needs with regard to light and noise, Ian is an early riser while I am a life long sleep-er in-er. There's nothing worse than finally getting off to sleep around five in the morning only to be woken an hour later by one's fully refreshed, annoyingly cheerful, ready to start the day with a run and a swim in the ocean, husband. Sleep deprivation is a well-known and very effective form of torture and for good reason. It's hell.

I reckon it's one of the main causes of society's ills and the world would be a much better place if all six billion of us got a good night's sleep on a regular basis. Solo sleeping may be unconventional but it doesn't have to be the end of all intimacy and affection. On the contrary. But what would people think?

There you go again, Sue, always more worried about what other people think of you than doing what's right for you. The worried part of me thinks, *What would my friends and family think if they came to visit?* I couldn't bear the sidelong glances and the judgement. Sleeping together is viewed in our society as a crucial part of marriage. Happy couples share beds. But what's the point in two bodies sharing a bed if neither of them is comfortable? Why put myself through the torture if there is a perfectly good spare bed available? And all for the sake of keeping up appearances.

It seemed to work very well for the French aristocracy. Sleeping apart was a sign of affluence for them. OK, so it may have come in handy for the King and his mistress but I'd live with that for a night of rest. I reckon that if we had separate rooms it would actually be good for our sex life. We could send each other messages during the day saying things like 'your place or mine'. It would be fun. It would be like dating again. Knowing that when we did get into bed together we'd be doing it purely to have wild, unbridled sex. It didn't have to mean the deathnell for all conjugal relations. We wouldn't be like Terry and June sitting up in their twin beds in their pyjamas and wincyette night gown drinking cocoa. I'd want my own great big king size bed to roll around in, with or without Ian.

Now, not to be put off, the dinner date forgotten, and wanting to make hay while the sun shone after all that darkness, Ian turned to me with a vaguely familiar glint in his eyes, a hint of hope on his lovely face and suggested that we both get an early night. Early night? It was only eight o'clock for God's sake – Ian never went to bed before ten. It took a while for the penny to drop. I looked at my in-pretty-good-shape-if-imperfectly-dressed-husband a little bashfully and headed for the shower.

Much as I'd like to be able to write a steamy sex scene to rival E L James' titillating prose, I couldn't possibly inflict that on you, dear readers. (I must confess to actually having read one of those books. A friend told me that every woman had to read them, so I followed her advice and read the first one, and while I found that whole red room set up very creepy and not just a little bit disturbing, I have to confess that I did find the book a little bit of a turn on in parts, unlike the film which was laugh-out-loud embarrassingly bad.)

Suffice it to say that an hour or so later I drifted off to dream land feeling like I'd just won the lottery, hit the jackpot, like the cat that got the cream, feeling like a new woman, and had the best night's sleep I'd had in ages.

You don't love someone because they're perfect, you love them in spite of the fact that they're not.
~ Jodi Picoult, My Sister's Keeper

Chapter 8

Write what should not be forgotten.
~ **Isabel Allende**

The next day was a Saturday and in my post-coital reverie I stayed in bed longer than usual, reliving yesterday's breakthrough and relishing my newfound feeling of well-being. It had been a long time since I'd actually woken up and looked forward to the rest of the weekend and the respite it would give me from work.

I've always enjoyed working, am passionate about teaching languages, and for most of my career going to work has been tremendous fun, but as life became increasingly frenetic and so much more complicated I'd lost my *joie de travailler* to some extent. When I joined the ranks of middle management many moons ago, in a previous century, a colleague had, not unkindly, warned me that I should expect to be 'shat on' (his words not mine) from above and kicked from below. I was scornful of his warning but he was absolutely right.

I've been lucky enough to work with some fabulous women, in particular over the last few years, but it is true to say that the people who have been most supportive and encouraging throughout my career have been men. I have no explanation for why this should be. My apologies to anyone who thinks I am selling out the sisterhood, but in my experience the sisterhood is a myth, particularly in the work place. I remember when I had Daniel, my male head of department, and the headmaster, bent over backwards so that I could keep teaching. My time-table was reduced so that I could work part-time, and I was able to rush home during recess and lunch to breast-feed. Fast forward a few years to my return to work after my second maternity leave and the work vibe couldn't have been more different. I had assumed, incorrectly, that being surrounded by females would make juggling work and parenthood easier. I was wrong. It was as if some – not all I must add – but some of my female colleagues thought *well I did it tough and so should she.*

    I've never been good at office politics. I just like to get on with my job. I'm crap at plotting and manipulating and jostling for position and I have no interest in empire building. I don't have a political bone in my body and I don't understand why some people seem to thrive on office politics, those sociopathic types who manipulate others for their own ends and will do anything to get ahead. I've met a fair few of those in my time but I've never been able to, or wanted to, play that game. If I had wanted to enter politics I wouldn't have become a teacher. Trouble is, I've always found it hard to stand up for myself or stand my ground. I get really, really upset at unfairness and have a very strong sense of injustice but I wish, oh I just wish, I was able to stay calm and poised, and be a bit more like Julie Bishop with her death stare and immaculate grooming.

    So on the morning after I realised I was on the way back, the day stretched wonderfully in front of me. My colouring in was up to date – I like to set myself goals so that I stay on schedule – Gaye was on a Buddhist retreat and Jodie had gone to stay with her mother in Canberra for a week to escape her horrible teenagers. Unlike mine, Jodie's children seem to do all they can to upset her and she has been in the Principal's office more often than Taylor Swift changes boyfriends.

What to do? I could work on that website I keep meaning to set up. The one that will make me a really successful blogger with millions of followers who will be on tenterhooks each week waiting for my latest masterpiece, filled with pithy observations and insightful social commentary, to be posted. Kind of like a western suburbs, middle-aged, female, more right wing version of Waleed Aly. Yes, that website, waiting in the ether to be created. I would make my fortune and we'd be able to put a double storey on the house we are renovating.

I like to do a bit of writing. As I emerged from depression, I found it really therapeutic to write things down, and began writing pieces about things that interested me. I even sent one article off to the Australian and it was published in the 'this life' section. I was so excited to see my name in print, but then I had a big crisis of confidence and self-doubt and not feeling worthy and I stopped writing for a while.

Then I began writing children's manuscripts and sent a few off to publishers. I received nothing back other than one very encouraging rejection letter. I was so happy that someone had written back to me and for once in my life I wasn't crushed by the rejection. I'm not good with rejection. I'm sure it all goes back to being replaced as a best friend by Marion Johnson in the Lower Fourth. Spurred on by this very encouraging rejection letter I sent off what I thought was a really good article to a magazine. Another response came back also rejecting my article but suggesting that if I had any others I could do some blogging. So that gave me the idea to start my own website. Trouble is, one year later I'm still thinking about it. Procrastination. The enemy within. Why do today something I can quite easily put off until I've found the perfect writing desk, lost those five kilos, rearranged the entire pantry and pared down my wardrobe into a sleek, streamlined arrangement of matching separates. Fear, that's why. Fear of failure. Fear of not being any good or having any talent, fear of ridicule, of trolls, fear of my own sensitive nature, fear of just about fucking everything.

Maybe I could write a letter to Ian, I thought. Before we were married we used to write to each other all the time. We met in England at the school where I got my first teaching job. When I arrived to start the school year in September, Ian had been working there as a gap student since January. It was a fairly posh English public school (read private if you are Australian) with beautiful grounds and a stunning tudor manor house set in picture perfect English country gardens where the Headmaster held a drinks party at the start of every term. All Pimms and cucumber sandwiches.

As I nervously approached the gathering I was intrigued by a figure walking along the path past the Chapel towards the drinks party. He didn't fit the profile of an English public school master. He was very young, very tanned with the most beautiful thick, longish, wavy hair. He was handsome in an interesting and unusual kind of way and he was dressed in the most immaculate Italian suit – he told me later he'd had it made in Milan during the Contiki tour he'd just finished.

We became friends. There were very few young teachers and we gravitated towards each other. It was not love at first sight by any means but we were drawn to each other and became really close over the coming months. I'd reached the stage in my life when I'd given up on men to a large extent. The previous year I'd left my catastrophic and incredibly traumatic first marriage (it lasted five months) when the emotional abuse I was being subjected to became physical. Low self-esteem again. I had been fooled for too long by proclamations of undying love, persuaded that extreme possessiveness was a sign of adoration, but one day something snapped inside me after a particularly horrific incident, and I left. I fled. Once I'd got over the trauma of leaving, and amidst intense feelings of guilt and shame at what I perceived to be a terrible failure, I realised I'd had a lucky escape and that power, control and abuse have no place in a loving relationship.

I went back to my old job in publishing for a while, and then decided what I really wanted to do was teach. I'd taught English for a year in France and it had always come naturally to me. My parents and two of my grandparents were teachers so it was clearly in my blood. Amazingly, I got the first job I applied for as a French and Spanish teacher in a really lovely school set in one of those so-very-English villages in north Essex.

I remember driving down the winding country road that led to the village that would become my home for the next four years and feeling that this was the start of something really good. And it was. I didn't become a teacher as a last resort, like in those hilarious Armstrong and Millar skits. I had come to realise that teaching was my vocation and it has served me well ever since that day sipping Pimms and meeting the man who would become my second (and hopefully last) husband. When I am in front of a class I forget all my insecurities and self-doubt. There is something very organic about it. It just feels so right. Of course there are difficult days, challenging students and some classes are better and nicer than others, but not for one minute have I ever regretted becoming a teacher.

So maybe I should write to Ian now, to try and capture some of the feeling of those early days, the days when we had to call each other from pay phones after he'd finished his gap year and was travelling round Europe in fine Aussie tradition. We wrote to each other on a regular basis and at great length and we spoke on the phone when we could. I mourn the dying, if not already lost, art of letter writing. There is nothing quite as magical as receiving a letter in the mail, all crisp and neatly addressed and filled with promise. I'd read and reread Ian's letters, cherishing all that he was sharing with me about his travels, his impressions of the places and people he was meeting. And always, he'd be missing me and looking forward to our next meeting.

I'd head over to France to meet him during our very long holidays – we worked damn hard during the term, including teaching on Saturday mornings, sport in the afternoons, boarding house duties, Chapel on Sunday. It was more than a job, it was a way of life and I loved it. I've always loved schools. As a child I devoured all those Enid Blyton books set in boarding schools and dreamed about being in the dorms having midnight feasts and pillow fights or scoring the winning goal in the lacrosse final against a rival school. I loved the descriptions of all the teachers including the proverbial heavily accented French teacher – little did I know that I would become one.

Yes, maybe I should write to Ian again. Write everything down to help clarify my thoughts and express how much I loved him and how grateful I was to him for standing by me while I fell into a million pieces. Our letters had sustained our relationship during those early years when we were apart for months at a time. When Ian's travels and our blissful reunions in France came to an end, it was time for him to return to Australia.

We parted one mellow autumn day at Heathrow. I thought I'd never see him again but for once in my life I didn't feel desperate or insecure. Ian was good for me and on top of our blossoming romance we were really, really good friends. We would keep in touch and somehow I knew that everything would work out, and that if we were meant to be together we would be. A few months later I was experiencing my first Antipodean Christmas with Ian and his family, then Easter, then a Perth winter during our long summer break. We knew by then that we would be together forever. I'd never been more certain about anything and I'm a terrible decision maker. I was once torn between two boyfriends who were good friends, so I went out with both of them for a while without them knowing, and of course it all ended it tears and I ended up with the wrong guy – the one I'd foolishly married and from whom I'd had to escape before I became another domestic abuse statistic. I'm still in touch with the other one, even though he lives on the other side of the world. We see each other every couple of years when I'm in Europe and I am extremely fond of him.

With Ian, it was just like coming home. We were written in the stars, fate brought us together, and any other cliché you care to mention. It started gently and grew into a deep love which totally transformed my life. I'd always thought love had to be turbulent and complicated. Now I had found my soul mate, just when I'd least expected it and it was as comforting and delicious as my favourite raspberry and orange crème brulée. And that's pretty damn delicious.

We had to spend more time apart while Ian sorted out his Australian citizenship – he'd arrived in Australia with his English parents, after ten years in South Africa, at the age of 11, and the family were British citizens. As soon as his blue passport arrived he came back to me. I was still working at the school where we'd met. He moved in to my little Elizabethan cottage, soon found work as a teacher himself and six months later we were married.

And now here we were in the autumn of our lives. I cast my mind back over the last few years. So much had happened. Both our boys were young men now. I'd lost my sister and both my parents, I'd battled crippling anxiety and depression, I'd experienced the suicide of a close colleague, and like every other woman before me I was trying to deal as best I could with menopause. I'd got through all of that and come out the other side. I'd somehow kept working but for a while now there had been a little voice in my head wondering if I should stay in my job. Was resigning an option?

We cling to our jobs and our salaries, we fear the uncertainty that might ensue, but what kind of life could I have as long as I dreaded Monday mornings? It was no kind of life at all. It was time to begin thinking about making some changes. I knew there was a long way to go, that this was just the beginning. I wasn't naïve enough to think everything would now be rosy. But that morning, for the first time in a very long time, I had hope for the future.

I made a coffee and went out to the courtyard. The morning sun was gaining heat and the warmth felt good on my face. I sipped my coffee and thought about the losses I suffered, the sadness I'd felt, the seemingly never-ending sense of grief and loss, and my descent into a deep, dark, crippling depression from which I thought I would never emerge.

But I was emerging, I would continue to emerge. I realised with a blinding clarity that I would be well again, and that I would stay well. And I resolved there and then to create something positive out of the darkness that had engulfed me for too long. I would not be a victim, I would use my experiences to become a better version of myself, I would seize the day, live in the moment. Retrieving a pen and notepad from the house, I sat down in the sun and began to write.

> *You must stay drunk on writing*
> *so reality cannot destroy you.*
> **~ Ray Bradbury, Zen in the Art of Writing**

Chapter 9

*You say you're 'depressed' – all I see is resilience.
You are allowed to feel messed up and inside out.
It doesn't mean you're defective – it just means you're human.*
        ~ David Mitchell, Cloud Atlas

In the weeks following the ironing incident Ian and I spent more time together than we had in a while. We escaped down south for a weekend and talked and laughed and remembered and felt lucky to have each other, and to have come through the last few years. In a weird kind of way I saw it as a test. A test of my newly-enhanced mental well-being, my newly-acquired self-knowledge and self-acceptance. I had a glimpse of the person I've always wanted to be, a person who wasn't held back by all the self-doubt and fear that had dogged me for most of my life.

Ian and I loved each other unconditionally – to the moon and back. He'd proved his love and devotion time and time again as he held my hand and dried my tears and stood by the side of a wife he must have barely recognised as the woman he'd married. I'd seen the pain in his face and felt his powerlessness to help me while I wrestled with my demons. But he had helped me, just by being there when I was so completely and utterly absorbed in my own head that I wouldn't have cared less if he'd had an affair, had several affairs. It would have been just one more meaningless and pointless fact in the meaninglessness and pointlessness of my existence at that time.

But now I cared. I more than cared. But in realising how much I cared I also realised that I was going to do all in my power to find out more about mental health and to make sure I stayed well. I would grow and learn and live a more authentic life. I felt an overwhelming surge of joy. Life was a gift and I wasn't going to waste any more time wallowing in the past.

Yes, life was a gift. It wasn't so long ago that I'd contemplated ending mine. It's so hard for me to write that, but it's true. I need to state it, and own it without shame. I was in such mental anguish that I simply didn't want to live anymore. I loved life, but I didn't want to carry on living feeling the way I did. And I genuinely felt that everyone would be better off without me. I really believed that.

I couldn't see a time when I would feel any better. I was tired of being trapped in my own head, tired of my racing thoughts, the painful memories, the grief, the sense of betrayal, the sense of guilt and shame and inadequacy. I truly felt the best thing I could do was to remove myself from the equation and rid everyone of the burden of having me in their lives. I read somewhere, in the aftermath of Robin Williams' tragic death, that suicide doesn't end the existential angst. It just passes it on to the next generation. I know that now, but at the time I couldn't see straight.

Depressed people are often totally self-absorbed. I was so absorbed in my own pain that I couldn't see the pain my family would go through if they lost me. Some people call suicide the supreme act of selfishness. Well maybe it is, but I don't understand how people can feel anything other than compassion for someone who truly believes their life is no longer worth living, and knows they can no longer live with their pain. It may seem selfish to others, but that is the nature of the illness.

I felt useless and worthless, and for a period of time experienced suicidal thoughts. They absolutely terrified me but thankfully I didn't ever get to the point of acting on them. I created scenarios in my head, but they stayed in my head. I have since discovered that such thoughts are not unusual; when you are in the grip of depression you lose your normal perspective.

Depression is so common. When it happened to me I felt so very alone, but now I know it is very common indeed. For a long time I felt the shame and the stigma that sadly still surrounds mental health issues. It doesn't help that every time there is a lone terrorist attack the perpetrator is often reported as having been mentally ill. The sensationalist and often insensitive reporting of mental health matters in the media does nothing to help reduce stigma or encourage open conversations. Gosh, I think, I've experienced depression and anxiety, does that mean I'm going to suddenly develop the urge to commit mass murder? I'm pretty sure that's not the case. I'm pretty sure that what I went through was the common or garden-variety depression and anxiety that seems to be increasingly prevalent in our time-poor, fast-paced lives — kind of like the common cold of mental health.

It can affect anyone at any time. It is part of the human condition. It's not a sign of weakness, and it's nothing to be ashamed of. I know that now. But for a while I didn't. I thought I was weak and pathetic and that everyone would be better off without me. Thankfully, media coverage does seem to be improving as public awareness increases and the community becomes more knowledgeable about mental health.

Recently, there have been some excellent, well-researched, sensitively-written long-form articles in our very own *West Weekend* magazine, an informative and thought-provoking read on a Saturday morning and a welcome, refreshing change from the tweets and soundbites and generally superficial content that dominates digital media.

Once I was past the worst I knew I still had a long way to go. Little did I know quite how transforming my recovery would be. I wanted to try to understand what had happened to me and why. I wanted to learn more about myself and find out if there was anything in my make-up or in my upbringing that led to me becoming depressed at the age of fifty.

I began to read widely, and I contacted *beyondblue* to share my experiences. That led to me becoming a member of their ambassador and speaker bureau. I now speak regularly at community and corporate events and have become passionate about raising awareness, increasing understanding and reducing stigma.

I've met all sorts of interesting people from all walks of life that I would never have met otherwise. It has been quite wonderful. It is no exaggeration to say that having depression transformed my life. It set me on a path that has led to a much better work-life balance, a renewed sense of purpose and self-belief, a deep appreciation for the beauty of our world, for love, friendship and family. I have connected with my spirit and found my place.

It is not a crime to be ill, it is not a crime to be depressed and it is not a crime to have suicidal thoughts. What is a crime is when the individual does not have enough confidence in their community to seek help without being looked down on or stigmatised.

~ **Jeff Kennett, Chairman,** *beyondblue*

PART TWO

lights on

Chapter 10
FINDING THE THREAD

As we are liberating ourselves, building new habits, and slaying our old habits — our own Minotaurs — it is critical to find the thread that works for us.

~ **Arianna Huffington**, *Thrive*

At this stage, it is important for me to reiterate that this is not a self-help book, not a how-to manual, but merely an account of my own experiences over the last few years. If, along the way, someone reads something that resonates, that will lead to greater understanding, self-awareness and better mental health, that will encourage someone to reach out and get the help they need, I will be delighted. But I am no expert.

Depression is different for everyone. There is no one-size-fits-all. It may last a few weeks, or several months, a year, or longer. I believe my depression was fuelled by my ever-growing anxiety and sense of being completely overwhelmed as I fell short of being the perfect wife, mother, employee, colleague, daughter, sister. Everything that had happened combined with my perfectionist nature, my shyness and introversion, my sensitivity to the opinions and judgement of others and my anxious disposition. All this provided the perfect setting for depression to thrive. My depression was a dis-ease caused by a set of conditions. Just as high cholesterol and clogged arteries can lead to a heart attack or stroke, or an excess of sugar can cause diabetes, the clogged thought-pathways of the mind, or the altered chemistry of the brain provide the perfect conditions for anxiety and depression to flourish. I have always been a worrier, with perfectionist tendencies, fearful of the judgement of others and overly sensitive to criticism.

Reading about depression has been pivotal to my recovery and the ongoing management of my mental health. Reading helped me to follow Ariadne's thread out of the maze and away from the Minotaur of my depression. Reading gave me knowledge, and as my knowledge and understanding increased, I found the power and the strength I needed and began to discover the tools and strategies that would help me to care for myself. In his book *Back from the Brink* Graham Cowan describes the different types of depression that are now widely recognised by mental health organisations. I clearly saw the type of depression I had experienced was called Nonmelancholic depression, which is the most common variety. It is typically a product of stressful events combined with the personality of the individual. The Black Dog Institute has shown that people who experience high levels of anxiety, shyness, self-criticism and high levels of interpersonal sensitivity are more likely to experience depression. Tick, tick, tick and tick for me.

In the same way that each person will experience depression differently, each person's recovery will also differ. Recovery didn't happen quickly for me, but once I had hit rock bottom there really was only one way to go, and that was up.

And up I went, one very small step at a time, sometimes wobbling, sometimes teetering and falling back to the previous step, but always, always picking myself up eventually and taking another and another tentative step. That's how I did it. Like a baby learning to walk. I fell on my backside, I got up. I ran into a wall, dusted myself off and changed directions. I put myself back together slowly but with increasing certainty that I could repair myself.

I don't regret having depression because it has shaped my life in a positive way. I wouldn't wish it on my worst enemy, but for me depression has been a catalyst for change. When I fell apart I was supposedly successful, in the accepted sense of the word. But depression jolted me into the realisation that I had to reevaluate the way I was living my life, that success needed to come from within.

While seeking professional help and taking medication are often crucial in the short term, there is something very empowering about taking responsibility for your own mental health and developing ways of managing it. In the first instance I consulted the health professionals, but as time went on I became much more interested in strategies and tools I could manage by myself without being dependent on the advice and expertise of others.

As a starting point, looking after my mental health meant being mindful of my triggers. A big warning sign is when I start to feel overwhelmed, when I find it hard to make decisions, and when my sleep is affected. Getting enough restful sleep is possibly one of the most important contributors to good mental health. Listening to your life is the key. I've learned how to read the signs my mind and body are sending me, and to act accordingly. If I am tired, I'll have a nap. If I feel overwhelmed, I'll take time out.

I needed strategies that would allow me to be well in body, mind, and spirit. For me, these three elements are interconnected and interdependent. In caring for the body, the mind is able to flourish, and the more the mind flourishes the more you discover the wonder and beauty of the spirit that resides not only in the universe but within us all.

In the following chapters I will explore some of the changes I made in my life. Doing things you enjoy is vital to recovery and they will be different for everyone. For too long I had neglected the things that give me pleasure and help me to thrive. A good strategy is to think of all the things you loved doing as a child, a teenager, or a young adult, and start doing some of them again.

Spending time outside in the fresh air is a great mood enhancer and nature is a powerful healer. Regular exercise has been clinically proven to improve mental health and staying physically healthy helps me to care for my mind. I refer to Martin Seligman who, in his book *Flourish*, outlines the often astonishing impact of exercise on mental well-being.

Walking is great therapy for me. On my worst days I still managed to drag myself out at least once a day to walk my dog. I love going to the beach, all year round, to walk and swim or just to sit and contemplate the ocean.

Yoga and meditation have also been very helpful tools. Listening to music is another of my passions and always makes me feel good. I love making playlists on Spotify of my favourite tracks – old and new – and workout tracks to play when I walk or go to the gym. I have also tapped into my creative side and discovered that I love writing and get lost in the sheer joy of it. I have done some writing for children and am in the process of writing this book. I also like taking photographs and would like to pursue photography further as a hobby. As I began to feel better, humour became an important tool in my recovery, and I discovered that comedy can be found even in the direst of circumstances.

It can be hard to slow down in our increasingly busy technology-driven world but I try not to rush like I used to, but rather savour the moment, engage fully with other people, and allow time to nurture close relationships and friendships. I have found that in being connected 24/7 through our mobile devices we often become disconnected from all the wonder of life going on around us.

I am a recent convert to Facebook, and love that I can stay in touch with friends and family on the other side of the world, but I'm mindful of the need to use it wisely and only post when I have something meaningful and interesting to say or share. As with all things, technology is best in moderation.

Reading has been a big part of my recovery. When I was at my worst I couldn't focus or concentrate properly for long enough but as I recovered I rediscovered the simple pleasure of a good book, and I now also read widely on mental health issues. Hearing or reading about other people's battles and struggles really helps to liberate it in me and reinforces the fact that depression and anxiety are nothing to be ashamed of.

Achieving a better work-life balance has allowed me to flourish again. I try to focus less on building up my superannuation and more on doing the things that I really love, and spending time with the people that really matter. I try to be grateful for every day and accept what comes my way, good or bad. I am letting go of the need to be the perfect wife, mother, colleague, employee, daughter, sister, and learning to be comfortable with my vulnerable, imperfectly human self.

> *... after I lost myself in the wilderness, in my grief,*
> *I found my own way out of the woods.*
> ~ **Cheryl Strayed, *Wild***

Chapter 11
FINDING BALANCE

Women need real moments of solitude and self-reflection to balance out how much of ourselves we give away.
~ **Barbara de Angelis**

One of the most challenging aspects of my depression was coping with the immediate impact it had on my working life. With the benefit of hindsight, this impact has been nothing but positive but at the time it seemed like an insurmountable problem. Over the last two years I have crafted a work-life balance that really works for me.

I left my job of fourteen years and stopped working as a full-time teacher three years ago. It took me a while to realise that it was time for me to take a leap of faith and look for new opportunities, seek out fresh pastures and find a new path. Achieving the perfect balance is something we all crave. I am fortunate that in the later stages of my working life I have the luxury of being able to work more flexible hours, and this newfound flexibility has been one of the keys to my well-being.

We spend most of our waking hours at work and my career has always been really important to me. Feeling useful, fulfilled and engaged at work has been proven time and time again to enhance well-being. As well as financial security work gives us meaning and purpose, but sometimes we cling to our jobs, believing that they define us and make us who we are, and we become very attached to our salaries, often to the detriment of the more important things in life. I had got to the stage where all I did was think about work. My depression made me reevaluate what I needed from my working life and led to a much healthier work-life balance.

I am still teaching, but on a more flexible basis, and I am now in a position to use my expertise to collaborate with colleagues outside of the classroom, which has opened up a whole new world of opportunity. Gone are the days when I'd be rushing from pillar to post juggling work commitments, school drop-offs and pick ups, feeling guilty all the time if I couldn't get to the boys' assemblies and sports days and collapsing in a heap after dinner only to do it all again the next day. After years as a full-time working parent, it is still a thrill for me not to have to get up and drive to the other side of the city every morning. That is not to say that I have ruled out working full-time again, whether in education or in any other capacity that may arise in future. I am open to each and every opportunity that comes my way.

I absolutely love teaching and I am genuinely interested in my students. The lovely thing about teaching is that you make such strong connections with students if you stay in one school for a long time. The relationships you forge with them over the years goes way beyond what happens in the classroom. I have been lucky enough to take groups to France on many occasions and the bonds made during those trips remain to this day. I am still in touch with many of my former students and over the last couple of years our paths seem to keep crossing in the most lovely way.

Just the other day while at the shops the girl behind the counter said to me, "Madame, it's Cassie, you never taught me but you gave us that talk about learning languages at the end of Year 9 and I was really hoping to have you for French but then you went on leave and never came back." We then had a lovely chat about this and that and went on our way.

That kind of chance encounter has happened a lot in recent times. I love coincidence and bumping into people when you least expect it. One of my students is friends with the son of a woman I became friends with after we met in India (more about India later). I only discovered when I was at her house, looking at all her family photos, and there she was, beautiful Tess. "I know that girl," I said. I'd taught her French through to Year 12, she'd subsequently kept studying the language in conjunction with law and spent time living in France. We are kindred spirits in many ways. She is a creative, thoughtful, sensitive, reflective girl. I kept bumping into her in the years after she had left school – at a yoga class, in Dunsborough, in the street somewhere in Subiaco. It was quite uncanny. And now, here she was in a photograph in my friend's home, and on top of that she has decided to pack in law, which didn't suit her personality at all, and become … a teacher.

She's joined the Teach for Australia scheme which fast tracks high-calibre students and often places them in challenging schools. And who has she turned to for advice about this courageous career change? Li'l ol me. We met for coffee while she was weighing up options and deciding what to do and now that she is enrolled in her course she sends me queries and questions and I am just honoured that she thinks she might learn something from me still. I am looking forward to seeing how her new career unfolds.

Another ex-student of mine has recently got in touch after reading about my work with *beyondblue*. I met her and her sister for drinks and we had the most wonderful evening. I also have my very own technology consultant – another former student I bumped into at the Apple Store in the city. For me, teaching has always been about the students; it is wonderful to meet them again and catch-up with their post-school lives.

Young people are funny and insightful and so very interesting. They help me to stay in touch with my inner child and keep a fresh perspective. Even the challenging ones, the difficult ones, teach me something. When I was at school it was a case of sit down, shut up, write notes, rote learn, put up your hand when a question is asked, do as I say and so on and so on. I had a good education in a very factual kind of way. I knew lots and lots of facts and I could write essays until they were coming out of my ears. I had the ability to memorise things really well.

I remember once learning over a thousand quotations for an English exam and I can still recite whole poems and passages from Shakespeare to this day. Rote learning is very out of fashion now. I believe there is definitely a place for it, as memorising things is definitely good brain training, but it shouldn't be the cornerstone of an education. I wasn't really taught how to verbalise my thoughts and question things. I didn't have the confidence to put forward my own viewpoint.

I was really really good on paper but speaking up in public was not one of my skills. I am by nature very shy, and as a child was painfully shy. My parents didn't help in this matter. As I was growing up, and particularly during my teenage years, I had a very strong sense that I was expected to tow the line and ask no questions. It was as if my parents were frightened of my ideas.

There was so much inside me that wanted to come out, but when I tried to express myself someone always seemed to get upset. I was often told: "Don't upset your mother." All I wanted to do was find out things or talk about how I was feeling, or get some comfort after being bullied at school yet again, but no one ever really wanted to listen to me.

I believe that teaching is still the most noble of professions, but it has changed immeasurably in the last two decades. When I first started out as a teacher in the UK I had a lot of freedom in my job. Everything has become so much more prescriptive, not just in Australia but worldwide. Each week I read articles in the *Times Educational Supplement* written by stressed-out, time-poor, completely disillusioned teachers, many of whom are leaving the profession they once loved because they cannot take it any more. I find this very sad. As teachers today we have little or no autonomy, we are no longer able to rely purely on our common sense to make decisions. Policy and procedure have to be adhered to at all times and absolutely everything has to be documented.

If you have a conversation with a parent, or a child tells you something, it all has to be written down. Neither of these things are intrinsically bad; at best they can actually save lives. But as we spend more and more time trying to keep up with all of the documentation and policies and entering data, as well as being in a continual state of improving ourselves, and less and less time actually planning lessons, doing research and marking – you know the kind of things that teaching used to be about in the good old days before

accountability and learning powered by technology and risk management and so on and so forth – we end up constantly chasing our tails and grow frustrated with our futile attempts to carve
out some space and time for ourselves within the work place.

Time to reflect and regroup is essential; it is during this time that we often have our most creative ideas. As we take on more and more, without any time being given back, this precious reflection time is eroded.

As teachers we tend to keep going and we are afraid to be seen to be complaining about our workloads as that would imply that we are not coping. We become teachers, not lawyers, or accountants or stock brokers because we value people more than money, and we always put our students first. But someone needs to look out for the teachers. So much time and effort is put into the pastoral care of students, and rightly so, but teachers work bloody hard and need to feel valued too. I sense, however, a change in the air. More and more schools are investing in the well-being of their staff, and long may it continue.

Recently, I received an email from a former colleague in the UK, who is on the cusp of retirement, in which he wrote, 'We managed (finally) to get rid of the poisonous deputy head, and have also lost … who was head last time you visited, I think. He's been replaced by … of whom I thoroughly approve: he believes in old-fashioned, or traditional values; and in letting people go their own way towards delivering excellence. That is unbelievably refreshing after years of scrutiny and form-filling. Still I guess you'd know all about that: I think Australia is even ahead of us in terms of bullshit in schools! (No offence!)'

I didn't take any offence whatsoever. On the contrary. I laughed, applauded, wrote straight back and we have a vague plan to meet in France in 2018. It should be so simple; 'letting people go their own way towards delivering excellence' says it all really. Give employees your trust and they will reward you a thousand fold.

On the topic of excellence, I will add a note of caution. It is of course the ideal to which we all strive, but we can't produce excellence or be excellent all of the time, every minute of the day. It's intimidating for employees, teachers, and students and simply not realistic. Clients will complain, parents might be disappointed their little darling is not achieving the promised outstanding level of achievement and overall remarkableness as a human being. We can, and do, strive for excellence but to expect that it will always be achieved is ludicrous. As Albert Einstein said, 'Try not to become a man of success, but rather a man of value.'

I'd taken some time off work after seeing my GP, but stubbornly insisted on going back to work before I was fully ready. It was a big big mistake. I urge anyone and everyone who is experiencing depression to take as much time off work as possible. That is easier said than done though. Many of us are programmed to believe that our jobs define us, and our identities become entwined with our working lives and our salaries.

Apart from those closest to me, no-one really knew what was going on in my head and how low I had become. I didn't understand it myself, and I judged myself to be unworthy, so it is hardly surprising that others may have done the same. I know now that judgement is often due to fear and a lack of knowledge and understanding. Depression can make people feel very uncomfortable, even those within our own families. People often just don't know what to say or do.

A year previously I had broken my arm and was in a cast for a couple of months. With a very visible outward sign, people couldn't do enough for me – they could see what was wrong and did everything they could to make things comfortable for me. But you can't see depression, you can't touch anxiety, there is no big blue cast around your head telling people that your brain isn't quite working as it should. In the same way, there is no big blue cast to take off, thereby demonstrating that you have healed.

Only when I accepted my condition, when I stood up, owned it, spoke about it and stopped judging myself was I able to deal with it and find my way back to health. I still find it hard to name it and speak about it, and I still feel the shame and stigma that exists in our society. But silence perpetuates the stigma of mental illness.

The shock and grief of losing a former colleague to suicide is difficult to describe. For a long time I wondered if there was anything I could have done to prevent such a tragedy. The relationship was not close enough to be recognised as 'bereaved' so it became a kind of invisible and unspeakable grief I felt I didn't deserve to feel. I had sat beside this person every working day for twelve years, but I wasn't either family or a close friend. But recent research tells us that so great are the numbers of people lost to suicide each year that most of us have been affected by it in some way. The sudden loss of someone with whom we have had a relationship has a profound, often life-changing effect.

The trauma I felt after the suicide of my former colleague coincided with everything else that was going on in my life, people dying and so on, busy busy busy, running here there and everywhere, jumping on planes at the last minute to get to England in time to see Mum one last time. I didn't make it. She died while I was in transit in Dubai. I needed my work to be a place where I had some control, some say in how my day would be, but the opposite was happening, and in the end I just fell apart.

I battled through the year before taking the year's long service leave that was owing. When the time came for me to return to work I finally realised that it was time for a more permanent change. During my year off I had thrived, reconnected with family and old friends, made new friends and explored new horizons. I wanted to keep that momentum going. We sat down as a family, talked about it at length and knew it was the best option.

I'd seen a couple of psychologists around the time of my original diagnosis but hadn't really clicked with either of them. I found myself just going round and round in circles rehashing the same old scenes. Two years later, while wrestling with work related matters and the implications of resigning from my job, I had a few sessions with a clinical psychologist who was recommended by a friend. I'd done some research and discovered that Dr Sophie Henshaw specialises in workplace relations, and, particularly, in helping professional women deal with stress and anxiety and find their voice. That's me, I thought. My anxiety was resurfacing, my professional confidence was at an all time low, I felt stuck, and was extremely fearful about the future. I found a YouTube clip of Sophie speaking on Channel 10 about workplace bullying and was impressed by the confident, articulate and intelligent woman I saw on screen.

When I met her, my first impression was that Sophie was a no-nonsense slightly awe-inspiring woman who commanded my attention in a nanny-knows-best kind of a way. But it soon became clear that she was so much more than that. With her expertise and a rare combination of insight, empathy, compassion and practical support, Sophie helped me to view my situation from a completely different perspective and to plan my way forward. She went above and beyond the call of duty and walked with me every step of the way. I was struck by her passion, commitment and genuine interest in my well-being. I've always been wary of being judged, so Sophie's non-judgemental manner was such a relief, and I felt free to explore aspects of myself that were confronting.

Over the course of our extremely intense but highly productive sessions, Sophie diagnosed me as having just below the clinical level of post-traumatic stress disorder, which was a bit of a shock as I thought PTSD only happened to servicemen and women returning from war and conflict, or people who work with the victims of trauma and disaster. But I now know that it can affect anyone and I understand how each person's reaction to a perceived trauma can be completely different. I refer again to Martin Seligman, one the founders of Positive Psychology, who in his book Flourish explains that PTSD is a combination of pre-existing conditions of anxiety and depression. He also describes how people who display intense depression and anxiety, often to the level of PTSD, are likely to grow in the long run and reach a higher level of psychological functioning than before if they seek help and are successfully treated.

At the time I knew nothing of the phenomenon known as post-traumatic growth and once again felt a deep sense of shame, but with Sophie's help I was able to manage my anxiety and come through some very difficult weeks without relapsing into the depression I feared might return. She helped me to work things through in my mind to the point where I accepted that for my own mental well-being the best option was to resign from my job. She gave me the safe space I needed and encouraged me to embrace my intuition and spirituality. Even though we only had a few sessions, the skill and integrity with which Sophie carries out her practice had a profound and long lasting impact on my life. She took the time to follow up with emails afterwards, and we are still in contact. She is a gem.

The fear I had been feeling about what the future would hold for me soon diminished. Once I had resigned I felt a huge sense of relief and on the very day of my resignation I had a job offer from a school where I'd always wanted to work. It was quite uncanny. Now, two years on, it was the best thing I could have done. I'd lost all my confidence, but until I resigned I couldn't see that the only way to get it back was find another path.

I've come to understand that this very important thing that we do – our work – has to happen in an environment that feels right for us, which allows us to function at our best and to thrive. I believe employers need to lead the way in mental health matters by showing their support and educating all their employees about mental health issues, no matter whether they are affected or not. Education is knowledge, and with knowledge comes the power to make a difference, and one day that workplace mental health awareness scheme may just save a life.

I read in the paper recently that in the aftermath of the suicide of a staff member, the WACA became the first State cricket association in the country to introduce a mental health and resilience programme for all players and staff. This year, I have been doing a series of talks at Bankwest to help raise awareness as part of their staff well-being programme. More and more organisations are recognising the need to invest in mental health training. While this is indicative of changing attitudes in our society there is still a way to go. It is only through education that we can improve understanding across all tiers of society.

If employers are fully informed about mental health issues, have sound practices and procedures in place, encourage discussion rather than promote silence, employees are more likely to feel safe and supported.

It sounds like a cliché I know, but once I had resigned and one door closed, new doors really did begin opening for me and opportunities presented themselves, often when I least expected it. It all now amounts to a work-life balance that really suits my personality and allows me to keep working while pursuing the activities that I love and that feed my soul.

Sometimes you just have to take a leap of faith. I feel very grateful and not a day goes by when I don't stop at least once and count my many blessings. I love the balance of my life now; I have a renewed sense of confidence in myself and in the work I do, and I am hopeful that I will continue to have new and interesting opportunities ahead of me.

Mental health has a direct impact on productivity and effectiveness at work. Creating mentally healthy workplaces is an ongoing process. Two years ago the Mentally Healthy Workplace Alliance teamed up with *beyondblue* to launch Heads Up, a national campaign for mentally healthy workplaces. The early signs are encouraging, with organisations investing in positive work cultures, mental health and resilience programmes, reporting better staff management of their own well-being and less time off due to stress.

Change has to be ongoing, and it has to come from the top. The blurring of boundaries between our working and private lives, largely due to the impact of technology, needs to be carefully monitored. Big round of applause to BMW and Volkswagen bosses for banning managers from emailing staff after working hours, and companies like Google and IBM for insisting that employees take time out, or the visionary Yvon Chouinard, founder of the Californian company Patagonia, whose motto is 'Let my people go surfing.' May many more follow suit.

We often simply don't recognise how stressed we are because being connected and contactable 24/7 has changed our understanding of what is normal. We see what everyone else is doing and we feel we have to keep up. But our minds are not designed to be on high alert all the time, and if sustained pressure and stress are not addressed, complete physical and mental breakdown can ensue.

Stress, unmanaged, can and does morph into debilitating anxiety, which in turn can lead to depression. Excessive stress disrupts our focus and distorts our perspective, which in turn causes difficulty in regulating our thoughts. If unchecked, it can have catastrophic results.

Take a rest; a field that has rested gives a bountiful crop.
~ **Ovid**

Chapter 12
FINDING CREATIVITY AND COLOUR

To be creative means to be in love with life. You can be creative only if you love life enough that you want to enhance its beauty, you want to bring a little more music to it, a little more poetry to it, a little more dance to it.

~ Osho

I never used to think of myself as a creative person. At school I used to dread art classes. I loved all the colours, I loved shapes and textures, but I just couldn't seem to draw anything very well at all. Tapping into my creativity, and discovering, in particular, the healing power of writing has been an absolute revelation. Writing anything in a work context has always come quite easily to me. I've always relished the opportunity to write a report, an article or a speech. And I'm the only person I know who doesn't really mind writing school reports.

These days they resemble short essays, such is the depth of detail we are told parents expect. That's bollocks in my opinion. All I want to know as a parent is whether my boys are trying their hardest and behaving well. Oh, and where they rank in their year group is also helpful, but not essential. Anyway, school reports trip off my fingers at a rate of knots.

I'm a fast typer, a skill I would urge everyone to acquire. It makes life so much easier. Not so very long ago I was still handwriting reports. Each teacher would have to write on the same report sheet, one after the other, and if anyone made a mistake, everyone had to start again. Technology put paid to that, but the downside is that we are now expected to write longer and more detailed reports and can lose sight of the fact that quantity rarely equals quality; more often than not a succinct and concisely expressed report would suffice.

So in the aftermath of my crisis, once my mind had stabilised to the point where I could string a few sentences together, I turned to writing to try and make sense of what was happening. This turned into some writing in verse for children. I'm no poet but I love the rhythm of language and can put a few rhymes together.

I've often written poems for friends or colleagues on special occasions. I wrote a poem for my mother at the end of her life and recited it to her just before I left to fly back to Australia after our final weeks together. I write to try and make sense of the world, to clarify my thoughts and understand myself better. I often write about past events. Living in the past is not a good thing, but sometimes we need to look back over our lives to understand how we got to where we are today, and to help us move forward with a renewed sense of purpose and a determination not to make the same mistakes over and over again.

I did that for a while. Writing saved me. It liberates me and allows me to express on the page what I have never been able to articulate with my vocal chords. I find my voice in writing. This is common amongst introverts who never seem to be able to find the right words at the right time. We need time to think before we speak. As I started writing, I remembered the diaries I used to keep as a child, teenager, and young adult. I reread them, and while there was no small amount of cringe factor, they did help me to understand and gain some insight into my younger self.

The signs were there early on – the sensitive disposition, debilitating shyness and lack of confidence that are common characteristics amongst people prone to depression and anxiety. My heart ached for my fourteen-year-old self. A desire to be loved contrasted painfully with my feelings of isolation. I always felt slightly separate and set apart, never fully embraced by my peers, never one of the popular girls, unable to confide in either my parents or siblings. I dabbled in angst-ridden, badly-expressed verse.

Decades later, writing once again gave me an outlet and helped me to make sense of the sadness that swamped me. It allowed me to escape for a while and brought a huge sense of release and relief. The simple act of putting finger to keyboard gave me a meaning and a sense of purpose each day, and the flashes of clarity it afforded were like finding the perfect pearl within an oyster.

I began to open and unfold. Writing gives me the luxury of time, to reflect, to gather my thoughts and to tap in to what I really feel, what I value, what I believe, what matters to me most in life. It has allowed me to work out how I want to live the rest of my life. In writing I become my true self. It doesn't matter to me whether anyone will ever read what I write. Well, maybe that's not true. Who wouldn't love to be the next JK Rowling? But seriously, I am already gaining so much from the act of writing, so even if no-one ever reads this, I would do it again a thousand times over.

Success aside, in the actual act of writing, in the process of putting thoughts and ideas into words on a page or screen, I go to another place. It doesn't always happen, but sometimes I simply get lost in the absolute joy of what I am doing, and I think this must be what is often described as flow. And that feeling is the best feeling in the world.

I read in Catherine Deveny's book *Use your Words* that you know you are a writer if you actually need to write to feel better. And that's where I stand. It's very simple. When I write, I feel better, my heads clears, my racing thoughts quieten. After a couple of hours writing I remain in a state of calm and bliss for quite some time afterwards. My family can tell when I've been writing, and also when I haven't. I get twitchy and irritable if I don't find some time in the day to bash out a few verses or pages. I've found that a minimum of two hours a day will do the trick. It's a feeling of achievement as well as a sense that I have moved forward in some small but significant way; that I have shifted something that was in my way. It's very difficult to describe but there is no feeling quite like it.

So I plan to continue writing. It doesn't have to be a masterpiece, it doesn't have to be a best seller. It could simply be a letter to an old friend I've lost touch with, or an email to a family member to tell them I'm thinking about them. When I was at university, and for some time afterwards once we had entered the world of work, my friends and I used to write long letters to each other when we had to go home for the holidays or when we were overseas. I recently came across a box of letters I'd kept from those times before the digital revolution. In one letter, from my friend Sharon who was spending a year in Mexico, I found an extract about friendship that she'd copied out from Kahlil Gibran's iconic book *The Prophet*.

CHANGING LIGHTBULBS

Reading it again – over thirty years later – brought tears to my eyes and I will treasure that letter until the end of my days.

I reread all my old letters. I hadn't realised how articulate we were, how well we wrote. They also gave me a renewed insight into my twenty-something self, with all my insecurities and hang-ups, but what really shone through was our zest for life, our youthful optimism, our hopes and dreams. *Gosh*, I thought, *I quite like that girl I used to be*. Maybe I am not such a terrible person after all.

I believe in the power of words, or pictures, or sculptures, or music to heal and change lives. I believe we all need to express what is inside us in the manner which suits us best. We all need to tap into our creativity.

Music is another passion of mine, and another one I neglected for too long. I learnt to play the piano and clarinet at school to a reasonable level, and for many years enjoyed singing in choirs. Now I mostly sing around the house, play the piano intermittently, but I listen to music as much as I can. All kinds of music, from classical to the latest hits. I love Birdy and Snow Patrol and Coldplay and Emeli Sandé and Adele and anyone who conveys emotion with their voice. Sting is one of my all time favourites and I've been lucky enough to see him twice in concert here in Perth. Just wonderful.

I don't mind a bit of throwaway pop either. I love that my boys think my Spotify playlists are pretty cool. I still find it amazing that I can create a Brit Pop playlist, or a relaxation mix in the blink of an eye, with a few clicks of a mouse and I thank the gods of technology for making all genres of music so accessible. Music moves me to the very core of my being. It sounds like a cliché but it's true. I heard an interview with Bob Geldof in which he said that great music makes him weep, in the same way that a great painting can move people to tears. And music is so evocative of the past, such a poignant reminder of defining moments in our lives.

As well as writing and music, I also love photography and as you already know I am a colouring-in devotee. I can't draw to save my life but I take great pleasure from bringing the outline of a butterfly to life by filling in the blanks. A friend bought me one of those colouring-in books and while I was initially sceptical it really does work. Like anything to which you need to give your whole attention, it focuses the mind and therefore forces you to be present and stay in the moment. I pride myself on never going over the lines.

During my year off I began to see colour as if for the first time. My travels to India and Spain were catalysts along the way. I'd been seeing the world in black and shades of grey for so long that when I arrived in India I was blinded by the intensity of colour all around me. The food, the clothes, the lush greenery, the plant and flowers, the vibrant spices and colours of the markets. In Spain it was the colours of springtime that lit up my world as I walked through the Galician countryside.

I've taken thousands of photographs over the last few years. Many of them languish on my computer but I'd like to start putting them into books or albums, or sharing the scenes and colours that so delight me on a website – that elusive website I am in the process of creating. I love looking at my photographs, and if they can bring pleasure to others that would be a bonus.

Now I try and be more observant of the colour that is all around us, particularly in the natural world. I've lived in WA for seventeen years but until this year I had never been out of Perth to see the wild flowers in spring time, so when a friend invited me up to her farm for a couple of days I jumped at the chance. We spent one whole glorious spring day exploring the flowers of the Wheat Belt. With her local knowledge, Jane knew all the lesser known tracks, and we spent hours just driving, walking a bit, taking photos, having a picnic. Just a perfect day, bursting with colour.

There is so much colour and beauty so close to home. I love the evening skies, when the light is fading and the colours range from muted purple to vibrant orange. I love the intensity of a blue blue summer sky contrasted with the red red earth further north. I love the changing colours of autumn, the reds and russets and yellows and oranges as the trees prepare to shed their leaves and make room for fresh growth. I love the pink and white apple and cherry blossoms and the magnificent jacaranda blossoms. I love the rolling green landscapes of the south west. It's all there and it costs nothing. All we need to do is look.

I love my set of colouring pencils, particularly when they are freshly sharpened and lined up neatly. While I have no artistic talent when it comes to drawing and painting I can appreciate great art. I tend to feel overwhelmed in huge museums such as the Louvre. My Parisian favourites are the Musée d'Orsay, if it is not too busy, and the Orangerie. I love the Musée des Beaux Arts in Lyon, particularly the impressionist section on the top floor. Each time I go to Lyon I spend a few quiet hours up there, and always leave feeling replenished, calm and uplifted.

Speaking of colour, I'm looking forward to creating a new colour palate for our house once the renovation is complete. I hear that grey is very on trend at the moment, but I think I might avoid grey.

Let me, O let me bathe my soul in colours; let me swallow the sunset and drink the rainbow.

~ Kahlil Gibran

Chapter 13
FINDING SILENCE

*Solitude matters, and for some people,
it's the air they breathe.*

~ **Susan Cain**

I've wasted too much time feeling like an impostor because of my introversion. When I read Susan Cain's book, *Quiet – the power of introverts in a world that can't stop talking*, it all made sense and a huge light turned on in my head. I wanted to jump up and down for joy in a very non-introverted way when I'd finished reading her book.

I knew that I was an introvert, that I was quiet by nature, but I'd often felt uncomfortable being that way. I can appear outgoing in the right situation, and I can party like it's 2099, but my default setting is to be quiet and spend time by myself. It was fine when I was on my own as a child, when I'd go off for long walks or bike rides in the countryside or when I spent hours sitting at the top of my favourite tree, or when I curled up with a good book on a rainy afternoon. Then I would escape into my own magical world of imagination and wonder.

But when people queried my choice to spend time alone, or my reluctance to express my ideas and opinions, and my quiet, shy, sensitive nature, I became very self-conscious. As Sophie Dembling aptly puts it: "I've been accused my whole life of being 'too sensitive.' This actually kind of pisses me off, but maybe that's just because I'm too sensitive."

In the same way that I was initially ashamed to have depression, I'd spent most of life feeling a kind of low-grade shame about not being more outgoing, feeling like a failure because I didn't enjoy big groups and often felt ill at ease in large social gatherings. I much prefer spending one-on-one time with a close friend to mixing with a bigger group (although this does depend to a large extent on the group).

While I've played team sport all my life, I don't usually enjoy those so-called team-building exercises that are sometimes thrust upon us in the workplace. I recently read that they actually don't do anything to improve morale, particularly if such activities don't suit people's personalities and if employees wouldn't normally choose to spend time together.

I also heard a report on the radio recently about the causes of stress in the workplace, and the number one reason cited was having to deal with colleagues, particularly bosses. Employees are individuals and need to be treated as such, valued for who they are – introvert, extrovert, ambivert or whatever they may be. The most effective way to boost team performance is to make sure every member has the resources and the conditions they need to work productively and happily.

As well as being introverted, I've always been super sensitive to other people's words, and easily affected by even just the body language, or facial expressions of others. My whole day could be ruined by a thoughtless comment, or a negative statement, a cold shoulder or a hostile sideways glance. At school I was teased a lot and when I tried to talk to my parents about it my father's response was to tell me "sticks and stones may break my bones but words can never hurt me."

I've learnt that sensitivity and introversion often go together. I've hated myself for being the way I am, and felt somehow less worthy than the more outgoing people around me, felt that I was a failure, a misfit. Reading Susan Cain's book allowed me to finally understand introversion, to realise I am not alone and, most importantly, to work towards accepting this part of me. It has been liberating. I think she is amazing and I'd love to meet her. She has since written a companion book called *Quiet Power, growing up as an introvert in a world that can't stop talking*. If only I'd been able to read that book when I was growing up, feeling like a failure amongst my peers, being judged for being too quiet. But 'if onlys' serve no purpose. I've read it now, and as my wise friend Julie says, everything happens when it's meant to happen.

Introversion and depression are not the same thing, although introverts may be more likely to develop depression. Extroverts often think introverts are depressed, because for them quietness would mean something was wrong. For us, quietness is the place in which we feel most ourselves. Many extroverts find it very difficult to spend time on their own and dread the prospect of an extended period alone.

Nor are shyness and introversion the same thing. As Susan Cain points out, Bill Gates is an introvert, but not shy. He is unaffected by what other people think of him and comfortable with his introversion. Not all introverts are shy, and not all shy people are introverts. Shyness is a personality trait that can cause discomfort and feelings of inadequacy in a social setting, so being a shy introvert is about as uncomfortable as it gets.

"You're so quiet. She's so unfriendly. Susan is so shy, she needs to come out of her shell. What's wrong with her? Why doesn't she want to join in? It's just rude! You're so sensitive. You're so emotional."

These were many of the things I've heard said about me over the years. I'm not rude. I have excellent manners, and I think I'm pretty friendly. I generally smile and say hello to strangers, and like to have a chat with the check-out person at the supermarket. I genuinely like people, and enjoy meeting new people. When I feel comfortable in a group I can be as outgoing as the next person.

One friend recently said to me, "You're so friendly and bubbly and outgoing." I can't remember what we were talking about, but I must have been expressing my discomfort at finding myself in a particular situation, and she found it surprising. She perceived me as friendly and bubbly and outgoing, as when she sees me it is always with a group of people and in a context where I feel very much at ease. So I can and do enjoy groups, but it has to be the right group.

Extroverts often make the mistake of viewing our quietness as a sign that something is wrong with us, and may perceive our need for alone time as very odd. In their minds, only someone who was sad would choose their own company over time spent with a group. But for an introvert, solitude is not the same as loneliness, and we can, in fact, feel very lonely when in the midst of so-called fun activities. Smiling and excitement and laughing can feel superficial if they aren't accompanied with real substance and a sense of connection to the people involved. This type of empty activity can lead to a cycle of feeling guilty about not joining in, and feeling overstimulated, exhausted and overwhelmed by everything that is happening around us. Ding ding ding! Big warning bells! Depression alert!

Some people do superficial conversation and forced smiles better than others. Some people feed off constant interaction with others, sharing mindless jokes, anecdotes, Youtube clips, and yes, food pictures on Facebook. They crave the limelight and need the attention. They get their energy from others. But often, these kinds of people suck the energy out of me. I read an explanation of the difference between introversion and extroversion. It is all a matter of where you get your energy. Introverts get theirs from within; extroverts get theirs from without. Introverts naturally gravitate towards their inner world and need time alone in order to recharge. Extroverts are more orientated towards the external world and gain energy by interacting with others.

Noisy workplaces can be challenging for introverts. I don't mind working in an open-plan office as long as everyone respects each other's space and has the courtesy to keep noise to an acceptable level. Any environment that leaves you feeling drained and bad about yourself is not the right place to be. Introverts value conversations and connections with like-minded people. We are curious about the world around us and like to find a sense of meaning and purpose in all we do. That is not to say that we don't know how to have fun, but we don't crave constant activity.

In a society that appears to value extroversion above introversion, I am coming to accept that for me 'seizing the day' sometimes means spending a quiet day on my own somewhere lovely and carving out my own little ocean of tranquility. Doing nothing much, and simply being for a while is often just what we need. No one ever told me this was an acceptable option. We don't have to be on a relentless treadmill of activity to live a full life. That is not the race we want or need to run.

There is a post doing the rounds on Facebook at the moment, showing a picture of a remote cottage and asking whether we would stay there for a month without Internet, phone, computer – any kind of technology in fact – if we knew we would walk out at the end with $100,000. Other than that, basic comforts would be provided. As my friend Suzette replied, "Hell, yeah!" Me too. I'd do it for nothing. I'd do it for six months. It is my idea of bliss.

Many introverts have spent their entire lives being told to do exactly the things that make them feel uncomfortable. I have no problem with the idea that pushing yourself out of your comfort zone can be a good thing. But to be constantly told you need to get out more and become more social, sometimes by psychologists who should know better, often has the opposite outcome to the desired effect by making us feel more anxious and withdrawn for simply being who we are.

Such advice goes against our true nature and basic instinct. As Aletheia Luna put it in her book, *Quiet Strength: Embracing, Empowering and Honoring Yourself as an Introvert*, 'If you are an introvert, you are born with a temperament that craves to be alone, delights in meaningful connections, thinks before speaking and observes before approaching. If you are an introvert, you thrive in the inner sanctuary of the mind, heart and spirit, but shrink in the external world of noise, drama and chaos. As an introvert, you are sensitive, perceptive, gentle and reflective. You prefer to operate behind the scenes, preserve your precious energy and influence the world in a quiet, but powerful way.'

One of the keys to any transformation in life is awareness. Finding out more about introversion has given me the knowledge and awareness needed to live my life the best way I can in a way that plays to my strengths. There will still be unavoidable situations where I don't feel totally comfortable, but I am getting better at managing them. I am trying not to feel guilty if I turn down an invitation, or leave a gathering early before I become too tired or drained.

I hope the stereotype of introverts as people who are unfriendly and don't like others will disappear. As LM Montgomery wrote in one of my favourite ever books, 'Matthew, much to his own surprise, was enjoying himself. Like most quiet folks he liked talkative people when they were willing to do the talking themselves and did not expect him to keep up his end of it.' We make up approximately one third of the population after all. We enjoy social interaction, but we experience it in a different way from extroverts. We are not misanthropists, but we prefer a small circle of close friends to a large network of acquaintances. Quality over quantity.

Living in a culture that values outspokenness and assertiveness over reflection and solitude can be tough. But introverts have much to offer. Our leadership style is more inclusive, less authoritative; more let's do this together, than do as I do. More what do you think we should do, than this is what I have decided. We are good listeners and great observers. Many great leaders throughout history, such as Gandhi and Abraham Lincoln, were introverts.

As Susan Cain states, 'Evidence proves that introverts make strong leaders – often delivering better outcomes than do extroverted leaders … Introverts tend to assume leadership within groups when they really have something to contribute ... they listen carefully to the ideas of the people they lead. All of this gives them a big advantage over leaders who rise to the top simply because they are comfortable talking a lot or being in control.'

As well as our ability to lead in a quiet and unassuming manner, our capacity for preparing and researching thoroughly as well as thinking things through, and our passion for the things that really matter to us, can make us powerful public speakers. Just look at Susan Cain's TED talk, which is one of the most popular ever, reaching over one million views in record-breaking time. I have found this to be true in my case. After a year of public speaking about mental health in a variety of forums, I have realised that I can communicate my passion, knowledge, and ideas quietly but very effectively.

While introverts do not automatically become depressed there is some evidence to show that introverts may be more prone to depression, simply because spending time thinking, analysing and reflecting risks becoming – in difficult circumstances and tough times – the type of destructive ruminating that can lead to depression. So we need to be careful, be mindful of our mood and monitor our thinking.

I am learning how to take Susan Cain's advice and spend my free time the way I want to, not the way I think I'm supposed to, or the way society expects. Introversion is not 'something that needs to be cured.' Neither introverts nor extroverts are better than each other. We are just different. I am hopeful that with researchers doing what they can to break down stereotypes and misunderstanding, we will all come to appreciate others' personality types, our quirks and behaviour, and be more accepting of people who are not like us.

Having described how extroverts can be draining to introverts, I need to add that some of my best friends are extroverts, and I love their positive take on the world. They complement me and help me to become more outgoing in certain situations. In the same way, they value my capacity to reflect, my independent nature, my ideas and my sensitivity. Not every extrovert is a draining bore, and not every introvert is a depressed loner. In the workplace, extroverts and introverts can complement each other well, and use each other's strength to reach a common goal. We need to embrace and accept each other's differing personalities, refrain from making incorrect assumptions based on outward appearance or initial impressions; we need to listen and learn from the quiet strength of introverts.

> *In a gentle way, you can shake the world.*
> ~ **Mahatma Gandhi**

Chapter 14
FINDING SPIRITUALITY

We are not human beings having a spiritual experience.
We are spiritual beings having a human experience.
~ **Pierre Teilhard de Chardin**

Millions of dollars are being spent and made out of the human race's dissatisfaction with itself, our constant craving for self-betterment, mind and life-altering experiences, miracle diets, detoxing, recharging, uplifting and the like. The wellness industry is rubbing its hands together at the prospect of all those middle-aged people seeking youth and enlightenment, people like me with a just a little bit more disposal income than we used to have – that is until we realise the cost of renovating our already perfectly acceptable suburban houses.

If you are re-doing your kitchen you apparently must absolutely have a scullery these days, and a butler's pantry. They are simply not negotiable. WTF is a butler's pantry? – I haven't got a butler. And a scullery – don't you need a maid for one of those? – this isn't fucking *Downtown Abbey* for God's sake. And benchtops – oh the agony of choosing a benchtop. You can forget laminate. It's got to be granite or stone, but what kind of stone, natural stone or engineered stone? Or that synthetic Corian stuff which costs a fortune that was so big about ten years ago and of which there are now so many brands, or you could have concrete or stainless steel.

So what would be the most authentic bench top I ask – I'm into authenticity – don't really know what it is but it sounds good. Well Sue, if you want the most sustainable benchtop you absolutely must go for the marble. Marble, I say? Sounds expensive. And would it be ethical? Oh yes, definitely ethical and it's really the only authentically sustainable choice you know. So that'll be $150,000 for a kitchen thank you very much.

Well you can just fuck-off then, I think with my $15,000 budget, which is still a shit load of money in global terms. It's a benchtop, it'll be covered in lots of crap and appliances and food and stuff and no-one will even care that it's authentically quarried Tuscan marble. Ah, well you see, that's the point of a butler's pantry – no-one sees all the mess and the authentically quarried Tuscan marble can take pride of place.

Choices – it's exhausting, do I go for the bog-standard builder's issue windows? Or, do I upgrade to the semi-commercial variety? Do I want sliders or stackers or bifolds? And what type of glazing? It's got to be energy efficient you know. Do I get the glazing that blocks out all the sun in summer, but then also in winter when you want it to warm up the house? What's that all about? It's exhausting. "It's a window, Mum," says my son, "first-world problem, Mum." And he's right. Those Kalahari bushmen seem perfectly happy without windows and doors and benchtops and sculleries and butler's pantries.

Despite my many misgivings about the wellness industry – or rather about some of the more ruthless members of the human race who jump on the wellness bandwagon seeking to profit from vulnerable, trusting people, looking to capitalise on our insecurities – I'm not averse to a bit of self-improvement myself, and as I was emerging from the hell of depression was as much in need of the replenishment of mind body and spirit as the next person.

While I've always loved church buildings, cathedrals and choral church music, I'm not what I would call a religious person – growing up in Northern Ireland ensured that in my mind faithful adherence to any particular religious dogma and doctrine equates to bigoted, narrow, small, sanctimonious, unforgiving and sometimes vengeful minds. I apologise to all those lovely church-going people who don't have a bigoted or judgemental bone in their bodies, but I haven't come across very many of them.

In the 1980s, when I was living in London there was a group called *Alternatives* that used to meet in a lovely old church in Piccadilly every Monday night. The whole New Age movement was all the rage at the time and really appealed to me and my friend Sharon, who'd always been a bit of a hippy at heart. We started going there in search of enlightenment and personal growth and found it to be a great antidote to and sanctuary from the excesses of the 80s of which I was rapidly becoming weary, and on which I was just about to turn my back to pursue a career in teaching.

Alternatives was an independent not-for-profit organisation that shared spirituality and new ideas with the local community with the goal of inspiring people to live more consciously, happily and, purposefully. On my last visit to London I went back to the church and saw that *Alternatives* is still going strong and has in fact become a landmark speaking platform for spiritual teachers and alternative thinking.

So in the dim and distant past, I'd explored different ways of seeing the world and better ways of living but as the years went by I'd all but forgotten and certainly neglected the spiritual side of myself. After my diagnosis with depression getting back in touch with my spirituality became a source of great comfort and joy to me that opened up a whole new world.

I don't like to take it all too seriously, and am quite happy to laugh at myself, but there is no doubt in my mind that developing an appreciation and reverence for all things spiritual has transformed my life. It all started one day when I was out walking my dog Ellie. I bumped into a friend I hadn't seen for a while. She'd lost her husband a couple of years previously – no matter how frustrated I sometimes become at Ian's lack of romantic sensibility, or fashion sensibility for that matter, at least my husband was still alive.

Karen is one of the most positive people I know. In the midst of her grief she threw herself into training for triathlons and also began to explore her own spirituality through Reiki, which gave her the calm and sense of perspective she needed after such a cruel and untimely loss. I'd always felt kind of guilty about not doing more to support Karen when she became a widow. Death is still such a taboo is our society in many ways. We never quite know what to say to people.

Karen and I weren't super close, but we knew each other through our husbands and boys and I'd always really liked her. She's one of those no-nonsense, tell it like it is people who is totally without artifice or pretension. She's one in a million and deserves the very best. Thankfully she had lots and lots of support from family, colleagues and friends, but I always felt I could and should have done more.

Anyway on this particular day as we were walking along with our dogs, I noticed that Karen was looking radiant. She had a kind of ethereal glow about her. Her skin was clear and her eyes were bright and she exuded health and well-being. She told me about the Ayurvedic health retreat in India, which had led to this transformation. India had never been on my radar as a travel destination, and I knew nothing of Ayurveda, but the idea of a retreat planted a seed. I was well on the way to recovery by this stage – it was a few weeks after my ironing epiphany and I'd definitely come through the worst of my depression – but I was still pretty tired a lot of the time and dragging myself to work every day was really taking its toll and preventing me from making the most of my new found sense of optimism.

The timing couldn't have been more apt. I was due to take leave the following year, had nothing planned, and the thought of having the time to simply be for a while, the space to gather my thoughts and the opportunity to rest, rejuvenate and regroup was very appealing. I was in dire need of a long and restorative break from routine. My aim was to become calmer, clearer, more centred and more connected. In short, to replenish my spirit.

As I walked back home, deep in thought, an old friend from my London days came to mind, and I felt the urge to call her. I explained that I was thinking of going to India and when she replied, "If you go to India, you must go to Kerala," I took it as a sign. I love signs and coincidences. Fast forward a few months and there I was, winging my way from Singapore to Trivandrum, on the threshold of an adventure that would completely change my perspective on life.

It is a bit of a cliché to say that I went to India to find myself, but I did in many ways, or at least I began to find myself and rediscover parts of me that had been hidden for too long. I learnt about the benefits of yoga, meditation and breathing techniques and explored my spiritual side. Spirituality is a very individual thing. For me it is best described as being a part of something bigger, something complex and mysterious, something beyond our everyday reality. I had become disconnected from that, so absorbed was I in routine and just getting through the day. I needed to slow right down and discover the bliss of stillness and silence, and Kerala provided the perfect environment for that to happen.

Being able to travel as I emerged from depression allowed me the space, time and altered perspective I needed. I wasn't escaping so much as retreating for a while, in order to return to my life better than before. Travel with intent is so very good for the soul.

Boarding the plane to Singapore, I found myself sitting beside a fellow journeyer. I had changed my seat on a whim while checking in online, and serendipity had prevailed. Ian always makes fun of my love of coincidence and frequent uttering of "it was meant to happen." Being a physicist who needs concrete proof before believing absolutely anything, he is a lifelong cynic. It bugs me sometimes. I want to share my belief in the power of the universe with him, in things being meant to be, but he just smiles wryly and says "yes Suze, sure Suze," with a slightly superior air.

Marie was a yoga teacher, a calm and reassuring travel companion. We spoke for a while about how and why we came to be travelling to the same retreat in Kerala and as I settled in to watch a movie I felt my spirits begin to lift and anxiety recede. A long stopover in Singapore provided time to connect with two other group members before we took the flight to Trivandrum, where we were met by Julie, our guide, and transported to our destination. There began one of the most transformative experiences of my life.

Our retreat was nestled in tropical gardens on a hillside overlooking the Arabian sea. During the group welcome on the first day we took turns to rise for a series of traditional blessings and greetings from doctors and staff. I felt profoundly moved and emotions began to well up as the tensions, grief and profound sadness of the past year rose to the surface. It felt like such a relief to be able to truly let go and allow my feelings to flow. Over the next two weeks I felt safe, respected and nurtured, and a blissful feeling of peace began to enfold me.

Learning about the Ayurvedic tradition was enlightening. I knew that it involved yoga, meditation and the harmony of body, mind and spirit but beyond that I was a novice. I discovered that this 'Science of Life' is a tradition almost as old as India's 5000-year-old civilisation. I have always been a little sceptical about alternative medicine, but I realised this was not alternative medicine to the people of Kerala, it was part of their culture. And science means knowledge, so who was I to doubt its efficacy. What better thing could one do than to improve one's knowledge of life? And the food was amazing.

We were given dietary recommendations based on our particular body type, our dosha. Food was plentiful, varied and delicious, prepared with great care, love and attention. We were greeted in the restaurant each day by Prasad, who took enormous pride in explaining the dishes to us and providing his own personalised menu suggestions, always with a beaming smile and a twinkle in his eye.

I love food. I'd completely lost my appetite for a while the previous year, which was most out of character. In Kerala, all my taste buds were stimulated and instinctively I began to eat more slowly and mindfully, savouring every mouthful. Of course, we had the luxury of time to do this. But there is a lesson in a slower more mindful approach to eating. Despite the abundance and being able to eat as much as we wanted, I never overate and always instinctively knew when I'd eaten my fill. Unlike at home where I often eat too much, or eat without really thinking about what I am doing. As we rush around in our busy lives we tend to never really know when we are actually full or when we are really hungry. Getting in tune with this was a revelation.

As well as the food recommendations, we were each assigned two therapists who would nurture us with a range of massages and treatments using organic herbs and natural medications. If you have ever had an Ayuverdic massage you will know they are very very oily. I have dry skin, so oil is good, but this was extreme. There was oil everywhere, my body was basted like a Christmas turkey, there was oil in my hair, pubic hair – I know it's not fashionable but I'm one of those women who likes to keep a bit of pubic hair – oil in my vagina, oil everywhere. To have a truly authentic Ayurvedic massage you have to be totally naked. And when you have the two-person massage there is no room to hide – arms and legs splayed, like Leonardo da Vinci's Vitruvian Man. Not for the shy and retiring, that's for sure. But it's so very relaxing.

Treatments took place in simple rooms on a special table made from a single piece of wood. Apart from the soothing massages – Ayurvedic massages use long strokes across the body rather than working on trigger points and deep tissue – my personal favourite was the Sirodhara, in which herbal oil or buttermilk is poured steadily across the forehead, inducing an indescribable trance-like feeling of peace, calm and oneness with the universe. The two hours spent having treatments each days felt like a unique gift to myself after too long feeling stressed, worn-out and filled with ennui.

So there I was in Kerala having my own little 'eat pray love' scenario, finding myself, all very lovely, if a little greasy. As well as finding myself I actually lost quite a lot of myself; about 5 kilos in fact. Half way through the retreat an optional day of purgation takes place. I took to the whole purging thing like a duck to water. On the first day I vomited profusely. My lovely friend Julie, who was also our guide, told me that this was normal and that I was starting to purge all the toxins and negative energy from my bone-weary body.

Julie is a truly spiritual person. Her life is devoted to the pursuit of enlightenment. She really lives and practises what she preaches. I sometimes don't feel worthy when I'm with her and could never hope to emulate the way she lives her life. As I said earlier, I don't like to take myself too seriously and am quite happy to take the piss out of myself as you have probably noticed. I think it's healthy and it makes me feel good. And the Dalai Lama laughs a lot doesn't he? Maybe he's not laughing about spiritual stuff, but he does seem to have a pretty good sense of humour.

Oh yes, I said in between retching, this feels so bloody great – not – get all that baggage out of my body, get it the fuck out. It could well have been that dodgy burger I ate at Singapore airport in transit but hey, purging all my negativity sounds so much better. Julie, if you are reading this, please forgive my flippant comments. You know I love you to the moon and back. I told you to go away while I vomited, but you stayed with me, you held my hand, you mopped my fevered brow. You truly were, and are, my guardian angel.

On the seventh day in Kerala – sounds biblical doesn't it … wrong religion – actually no, come to think of it Kerala is one of the few places where Christians, Hindus and Muslims manage to live in harmony. Anyway, on the seventh day an optional purgation takes place. An interesting-looking, rather pungent medicine is administered to induce said purgation, which would occur gently and naturally and produce amazing feelings of lightness and well-being. In other words we would spend the whole of the next day shitting as if there was no tomorrow. Just when you thought it was safe to leave the toilet bowl, more would come out, and it just kept coming. So by the eighth day I had lost so much of myself what with all the vomiting and shitting, and felt as light as a feather.

I proceeded to glide through the second week, feeling cleansed and just a little bit pleased with myself. Not so much 'eat pray love' but rather vomit, eat, shit, and then shit a bit more, but oh it felt good. I definitely shifted a lot of negative stuff in Kerala and did indeed have an amazing feeling of release and lightness. They know a thing or too those Ayurvedic doctors and lovely people of Kerala.

Equally transformative was the wonderful sense of being safe for a while, and I seemed to be purging naturally, almost unconsciously, in this haven far from the chaos of everyday life. I felt soothed by the kind therapists whose smiles spoke a thousand words, and fell easily into the rhythm of the day. Some days I would cry, simply out of a sense of release and relief after all the years and months of tension. The therapists would say to me "Why you cry Miss Sue? Be happy Miss Sue," and I saw that it really was that simple.

Despite having very little in the material sense these kind and gentle people were always smiling and they chose to be happy. I, too, could choose to be happy. I could stop wallowing and rehashing and drowning in my own angst. It was humbling. Time became my companion rather than my enemy, everything slowed down and became more vivid. My sense of smell, of touch, of sound grew clearer as I began to savour the moment, freed from the need to rush to keep up with daily demands without stopping to really enjoy the present.

As a confirmed introvert I'm not a big fan of group holidays but Julie had assured me that this was a group holiday for people who don't like groups, and so it was. Any fears I had about being judged for being too quiet or keeping to myself proved to be completely unfounded. I felt totally integrated and accepted within the group as everyone had a respectful awareness that we were all on our own journey. It was refreshing to realise that it wasn't until the fourth or fifth day that we discussed our working lives, and even then, only in passing.

Conversations were honest, open and frank. No-one felt compelled to speak for the sake of it. We didn't really do small talk. There was none of the grandstanding or one-up-person-ship that pervades our modern lives. Sometimes people chose to sit separately in the restaurant or take lunch back to their cottage. As time went on I began to confide in my newfound friends, secure in the knowledge that whatever I had to say had value and merit because it came from my heart, and that I would be listened to without judgement.

An early morning guided meditation set the tone for each day. Every meditation was carefully thought out and planned to capture a particular emotion or need within the group, ensuring that we began each new day feeling inspired, but also challenged to look inside ourselves at the deepest level. Meditation was followed by Pranayama breathing on a grassy terrace above the beach as the fishermen hauled their catch and women waited expectantly to see what they could sell in the markets that day, knowing that their livelihood depended on the size of the catch. In the afternoons I would often join the beginners' yoga class, a restorative and rejuvenating practice which slotted perfectly into the gentle rhythm of my days.

Meditation has been an absolute revelation for me and two years on I still try to incorporate some kind of quiet time into my daily routine. You don't have to have a shaven head and wear orange to meditate. You can do it anywhere. I often spend time at the beach simply contemplating the ocean and find that really helps to clear my mind. You can do it cross-legged if you like, or lying down, or sitting on a chair. You can do it listening to music or not, outside or inside. There are no rules as far as I am concerned. The key is to give yourself time each day to switch off your thoughts and focus the mind.

In between scheduled classes and treatments, I spent time lying in my hammock, just contemplating and being. I wandered around the beautifully kept gardens filled with spring blossoms, birds and butterflies; I watched the skies at sunset through the swaying palm trees. After dinner, some of the group would wander through the village outside the retreat, chatting to the shopkeepers over a cup of tea, buying clothes from the tailors and beautiful rings or bracelets from the jewellers.

During the second week I began to wander farther afield, up the village street, finding myself one day in a local market where fruit, vegetables and fish were sold. Surrounded by myriad colours and smells I stayed a while, observing the simplicity of the everyday life of these gentle people. I spent one tranquil afternoon floating lazily along the labyrinth of waterways that make up Kerala's emerald backwaters, stopping in remote villages where women washed their clothes and dishes, while children ran along the banks, waving and smiling at passers by.

It sounds a bit too perfect perhaps, but it really was. Two weeks of tranquility and stillness worked their magic. Freed from the intrusion of phones and the expectation to be connected 24/7 the mind unwinds and finds itself again. The challenge is to sustain this feeling back in the real world, to apply what has been learned, to keep the momentum going. Time has moved on since my year off, a year in which my trip to Kerala set the tone for the replenishment of my spirit, and two years on my life remains transformed. Of course challenges arise each day, every week, and my serenity is often tested when routine takes over and obstacles appear. When I can't get to grips with the latest IT update, when that driver in front of me fails to merge or indicate; but the lessons I learned on Kerala's sacred earth continue to sustain me.

I am still prone to anxiety but I now have the tools to manage it more effectively. The practice of yoga, meditation and mindfulness forms an integral part of my week and I have a deep appreciation for the importance and bliss of stillness. The short time I spent in Kerala helped me to rediscover my zest for life and the joy of simply being. It gave me a renewed gratitude for the love of my husband and children, for genuine friendship, for the beauty of nature and for a material abundance far beyond the wildest dreams of many on this earth. I have remained connected with the people I met in Kerala, and the new friendships I have made are affirming and genuine, cemented by a shared quest to remain true to ourselves, to dwell less on the past and avoid needless fretting about the future.

So there is it. My two weeks of eating and praying and pooing and puking in south west India had a profound impact, not just on my mental health but on the way I choose to live life. There will always be obstacles and stresses, of course, and there is no such thing as a pain-free existence. But sometimes the obstacles in our way are the very things we need to get where we want to go.

My short but very intense two weeks in Kerala transformed my perspective and will remain with me always. I began to find myself in India and I'm finding myself just a little bit more every day. I wonder where Indians go to find themselves? Have you ever thought of that? Where do the lovely people of Kerala go if they want a break from all that oil and enlightenment and positivity and happiness? How about they come and find out what it's like to spend just another day in WA? Just another day when no-one bothers to indicate, or if they do it's brake first giving the car behind no warning whatsoever, slow down to an annoying and unnecessarily low speed, and then maybe, just maybe, an orange light will flicker momentarily as the vehicle makes its turn at an excruciatingly slow pace.

And what about merging? No-one seems to master the art of merging, so it takes us twice as long as it should to get home on the freeway to our newly renovated houses with our butler's pantries and sculleries. That would test your level of enlightenment oh peaceful calm people of Kerala. Come and spend a day in WA and you'll be racing back to your ashrams with a new found appreciation for life. I jest, of course. WA is a great place to live, despite the terrible drivers.

There is a light in this world. A healing spirit more powerful than any darkness we may encounter. We sometime lose sight of this force when there is suffering, and too much pain. Then suddenly, the spirit will emerge through the lives of ordinary people who hear a call and answer in extraordinary ways.
~ **Richard Attenborough**

Chapter 15
FINDING YOGA

*Yoga: a Hindu spiritual and ascetic discipline,
a part of which, including breath control, simple meditation,
and the adoption of specific bodily postures,
is widely practised for health and relaxation.*

When I got back to Perth I set out to find the perfect yoga class in order to continue my new, enlightened existence. So on the advice of a friend I rocked up to my one and only Bikram yoga class. What's that all about? Bikram yoga. Hot yoga. It's 38 degrees in Perth for six months of the year – well that's an exaggeration but it's pretty bloody hot in summer, and this was summer – and people were choosing to enclose themselves in a hot, airless 38-degree room.

The first thing I noticed was the wall of mirrors in front of us, and the number of lithe, young bodies warming up while gazing admiringly at their own reflections. I may have a perfectly coordinated wardrobe of very eye-catching active wear but I don't want to have to look at my imperfectly shaped body while I attempt to adopt a series of gravity-defying postures. I don't want to see my contorted limbs and my distorted bright red face thank you very much. I want to focus on my inner beauty not my external imperfections.

Excuse me people, I wanted to shout, I've been to India, and there are no mirrors in yoga. Please remove. But I didn't. I tried, I tried my best, I really did, but I couldn't keep up. Go into child's pose, the instructor kept telling me, clearly seeing that I was so far out of my comfort zone I was floating around in space with George Clooney and Sandra Bullock. Just keep breathing and stay in child's pose. *Of course I'm going to keep breathing you stupid bitch* (sorry, that's not a very yogic word), I thought, I'd be dead otherwise, and while your class is torture and nothing like the yoga I practised in Kerala, I'd like to stay alive thank you very much.

And then, horror of horrors, I felt a purge coming on. All that purging in India must have programmed my body and I felt the beginnings of a big vomiting session rumble in the depths of my tummy. I retched. I stood up. No, no, yelled Samara, or Tamara or Juniper or Sheridan or whatever the fuck her name was. Why are there no yoga teachers called Janet, or Jeff, or Jane or Anne? Why do they always have to be called something a bit trendy or a bit exotic? I bet they make their names up. I bet most of them are called Doris or Pat really. Anyway, I ignore the command of Doris, AKA Samara, and ran to the door. No no, she yelled, you can't open the door, you'll break the energy seal. *Fuck your energy seal,* I thought as I ran into the reception and vomited all over the authentically ethically-made rug, the door banging behind me. There was no one in reception. Everyone was in the hotbox with the now contaminated energy I'd left in my wake.

I finished retching and straightened up. There was a shelf unit filled with freshly laundered perfectly white towels and, I am ashamed to say I derived no small amount of satisfaction from wiping up the results of my purging with a couple of the towels. I did a pretty good job with the rug and I wrapped the towels up carefully and put them to one side. I sat down and drank some water. After five minutes or so Doris/Samara deigned to come out, to see how I was I assume but I can't be sure because she didn't ask. Rather than enquire as to my well-being, she looked most displeased as she looked me up and down, noticing, I have no doubt, that my carefully chosen active wear was in last year's colours and not remotely on trend.

"It's always hard the first time," she said condescendingly, "you have to push through and it will get better," she continued patronisingly.

"I have never felt so uncomfortable in my life," said I, "this is not what yoga is about as far as I am concerned. Yoga should be nurturing and comfortable and accepting, not judgemental."

I was going to tell her about the vomit, I really was, but when she looked me up and down one more time and added snootily, "well it's not for everyone, perhaps some people just aren't up to it," I just walked out. Leaving her to discover for herself the remains of my intestinal tract.

I tried restorative yoga next. It's so lovely. You just lie around a lot in slightly different positions in a pristine white studio with beautiful floorboards and they cover you up with nice blankets and give you big bolsters and sometimes even cover your eyes with a lovely soft bean baggy eyepatch. Not a lot of exercise going on there. You won't be tightening up your pelvic floor doing restorative yoga but it's lovely and floaty and dreamy and they play lovely floaty dreamy music.

I did a session of ten classes then I realised I was paying $30 an hour to lie down and listen to music. So I tried a few other yoga classes. Some were really lovely, and some I found quite intimidating. Some were kind of a yoga/pilates fusion, some focused more on the spiritual than the physical, and for some the spiritual was just an afterthought.

I used to be really intimidated by all the beautiful bendy flexible people who do yoga. Sure, there may have been an element of jealousy there too – I'd love to be beautiful and flexible and bendy. There was, for a few years, a very nice yoga studio in the south west of WA where I always went when I was down there on holiday. It was full of the aforementioned beautiful bendy people, and I always felt like something of an impostor, but I liked it anyway. It went well with the relaxed holiday vibe in that part of the world. And then one day, it had closed down. It was no more. I subsequently found out that there had been some kind of a partner swapping type of thing going on amongst the oh-so-enlightened owners of the studio. I didn't find out the details but apparently keeping the business going became untenable. It gave a whole new meaning to the downward dog position and kind of exploded the myth I'd created in my mind that people who do yoga are better than everyone else.

Yoga has become big business here in the west and some might argue that it is has become something of an elite practice for the Lexus-driving yummy mummies in our wealthier suburbs. Certainly, the proliferation of yoga studios in such suburbs would seem to add weight to this argument. But there are many ways to practise yoga. It doesn't have to be in a chic studio fitted out in the latest interior design trends. On the contrary, school halls and community centres can easily become impromptu yoga studios and practising yoga outdoors in parks or by the beach adds a whole extra dimension to the experience.

Big business or not, and there will always be those seeking to exploit something for their own gain, when mainstream medical journals such as the Lancet in Britain espouse the benefits of yoga, there can be no doubt as to its efficacy. It is not uncommon for GPs to suggest yoga to patients experiencing a range of ailments, in particular stress, anxiety and depression, but also back and muscular pain.

The CEO of Yoga Australia, Shyamala Benakovic, claims yoga can improve many aspects of your physiology and psychology, and as a mere novice practitioner I find this to be true. I found that as my body began to open and become more flexible, my mind also unfolded and expanded, and I feel a tangible reduction in stress and anxiety levels after even just a short session.

The trend for posting seemingly impossible yoga poses on social media flies in the face of what yoga is all about. One of the intentions of the practice of yoga is to transcend the ego, not feed it, so posting a photo of yourself with your ankles round your ears most definitely runs contrary to the practices and beliefs described in the Bhagavad-Gita, the most renowned yogic scripture. You don't have to be able to stand on your head to understand the true meaning of yoga. I must say though, I'm pretty damn good at standing on my head – been doing it since the age of seven – who knew I was already a yogi at such a tender age?

My brother recently sent me all my parents' old slides – thank you dear brother – and there I was, fourteen-year-old me, standing on my head on one of the beautiful beaches in the west of France. Maybe I should post that on Facebook. No, Sue, no you absolute hypocrite, what were you just saying about ego?

Yoga classes aside, I decided that I could create my own little oasis of calm and loveliness in my own home. I have my mat and my bolster and my Tibetan singing bowl carefully placed on a table with my Buddha statue and some incense sticks, and I bliss out for a while each day. The essence of my practice is about being in stillness, quietening the mind, and taking the time to experience a little peace and tranquility in this mad mad world.

> *Yoga teaches us to cure what need not be endured and endure what cannot be cured.*
>
> **~ B.K.S. Iyengar**

Chapter 16
FINDING STILLNESS

*Attention to now is absolutely precious.
It does more than liberate us from past events;
it delivers us to our life in the present ...
the original events will not have changed, but you will.*

~ Stephanie Dowrick

Mindfulness is very much a word of the moment. It is pretty simple really. We have become so clogged up with the frantic pace of our lives that we rarely find the time to just be present in the here and now, to pay full attention to what we are doing, and be still. We are too busy thinking about what we need to do next, or what we forgot to do this morning. It sounds simple but it is easier said that done, and it takes practice.

But the brain can be trained to become more attentive, even just for half an hour a day, and that process of slowing down the racing ruminations of the mind really does work. If you are in any doubt about this, you should read Norman Doidge's book *The Brain That Changes Itself.*

I have never been afraid of silence, in fact it's something I cherish and crave, and I have no problem sitting still. The difficult thing for me is taming the monkey mind, as they say in yoga. That endless chattering in your head that won't leave you alone. It goes hand in hand with the idea of changing your thinking. You can't necessarily stop all negative and destructive thoughts coming into your mind, but you can go a bloody long way to just telling them to fuck right off.

When I was in Kerala – that sounds very Ab Fab doesn't it – when I was in Keraalaa Daahling, all said with those peculiar vowels that seem to abound in the wealthier echelons of Melbourne society and the Mornington Peninsula. Wonderful place. Ian and Ben and I had a great holiday there in a friend's beach house – we choose our friends wisely you know. Actually, we had no idea they had a beach house when we met them in Melbourne and were beyond grateful when they kindly offered us the use of what was actually a very splendid residence with panoramic views all around the aforementioned peninsula.

Anyway, getting back to Kerala darling, as well as all the treatments and purging and yoga and general loveliness that abounds there, we were taught how to do Pranayama breathing. One psychologist I saw told me that my normal resting breathing rate was twice as fast as it should be. This is very common in people with an anxious disposition, and clearly something I needed to work on, so I took to the practice of Pranayama like a duck to water.

Our teacher was one of the most gentle, serene men I have ever met. He was also a yoga master and had won many awards, but he was an unassuming, humble person with a beautiful, quiet aura that I could almost see. Mr James was his name. He wore plain, long, trousers and a normal shirt when teaching yoga or Pranayama. Just like the serene young woman who took our beginners' yoga classes in the afternoons, fully clothed in the most beautiful traditional Indian dress, which impeded her movements not one bit.

Unlike the nightmare of Bikram yoga, this yoga was calm and quite still and very, very quiet. No barking of instructions. Just gentle demonstration and a few words here and there to clarify what we were doing. Not a piece of fluorescent active wear in sight. Oh, we have got yoga so wrong here in the west.

Back to breathing. We had been told about the practice of Pranayama prior to arriving at our health resort, and I have to confess that I was a little sceptical, as is my wont. But when I sat down on the grassy terrace on the first morning and began the series of exercises, after we had been guided through our first meditation by Julie, I felt immensely soothed. For the uninitiated, Prana means 'vital energy' or 'life force' and Ayama is defined as 'extension' or 'expansion.' By practising Pranayama we can help maintain mental balance, cleanse our nasal passages and strengthen the lungs and the respiratory system. It claims to reduce bronchial congestion and asthma, and also to tone and strengthen the abdominal organs and muscles.

Well, I am an asthma sufferer, and since I started focusing more on my breath, I can count on one hand the number of times I've had to use my inhaler. And that from someone who used to puff away on a ventolin several times a day. It may be a coincidence, but I doubt it. It further claims to induce a higher state of vibratory energy, concentration and awareness. I am not sure what vibratory energy is, but I can attest to feeling clearer, more focused, more aware and generally really alive after a pranayama session.

We learnt to do a sequence of exercises, but you don't have to do them all at any given time. One of the best known is alternate nostril breathing, which is sometimes incorporated into yoga classes. Regular practice of Pranayama is said to reverse the aging process and help maintain optimal health. What's not to like? I need to do it more often. Mr James allowed us to record his class, so I can listen to him and join in anytime – complete with the birds singing and the waves crashing on the shore below the grassy terrace in the background. Writing this has made me want to sit down and do it right here right now.

Whether it is through the practice of Pranayama, or other simple exercises, of which there are many, focusing on the breath is the first step to becoming more mindful. It's all part of meditation as well. All these practices are intertwined. If you focus on the breath, you will become more mindful, and if you become more mindful you are well on the way to meditating.

Focusing on breathing creates a bridge between the body and the mind, and helps manage the destructive thoughts, the rehashing of the past and fear about the future that are so common with anxiety-driven depression. You can't breathe in the past or the future, so it is an excellent way to stay mindful and present and embrace stillness. It takes time but it works.

When the mind wanders, bring it back to your breath. I don't always remember this, but whenever I do, it brings me back to my centre. More and more people are incorporating yoga, meditation, and mindfulness into their lives; even fifteen minutes of quiet time each day helps to calm the mind.

I read an interview with Hugh Jackman in which he said, "Some of the clearest ideas or epiphanies I've had in life happened during or after meditating. Everything becomes clear and the truth comes out."

If it's good enough for Hugh it's good enough for me.

> *If you want to conquer the anxiety of life,*
> *live in the moment, live in the breath.*
> **~ Amit Ray, *Om Chanting and Meditation***

Chapter 17
FINDING THE WAY

All truly great thoughts are conceived while walking.
*~ **Friedrich Nietzsche***

Towards the end of my retreat in Kerala I found out that Julie's next trip involved walking part of the *Camino de Santiago* in Spain. And so it was that I found myself on a plane bound for Barcelona, not much more than a month after returning from Kerala, to experience my second, equally wonderful, spiritual journey. Lucky, lucky me!

My initial reaction when I discovered there was one place left on the trip was that I couldn't possibly go, and the guilt kicked in about leaving my family yet again. But do you know what? It was Ian, my lovely Ian who told me that I had to go. He'd seen the transformation in me when I returned from Kerala. It was my year off, my year to recharge and reboot and "you should bloody well do it, Sue," said he. What a man.

It was in Kerala that I'd started writing a journal and began to appreciate the therapeutic effects of finding my words. True to my earlier reminiscing about the letter writing days of our courtship, I'd also written a long letter to Ian and presented it to him when I got back to Perth. It was the beginning of me finding my voice again, making sense of everything that had happened and becoming more comfortable in my own skin.

I realised how lucky I was to have the freedom, and the funds to travel. It was interesting seeing the mixed reactions my journeys in 2014 elicited. I'd get incredulous comments like "You're going to India, on your own?" or "You're off again, how will Ian and the boys manage without you … again" or "My husband would never allow me to do what you are doing." Comments mostly from women, comments that seemed to be judging me as selfish or irresponsible or downright neglectful. I rest my case about the sisterhood.

Given how conditioned we are by society, part of me did feel a little guilty about giving myself time out and spending money on myself. Ian and I are not extravagant people. Neither of us likes shopping, and neither of us care about designer labels and the latest fashions. We enjoy food but prefer cooking something lovely at home. We enjoy wine but don't drink to excess. We have managed to give our boys a private education but we fly economy, not business class. We have never bought a new car. It sounds as though I am trying to justify myself – maybe so. I am aware that not everyone who has been depressed is able to do what I did. But to put it in context, I had worked full-time for the best part of 25 years, and the year's leave was accrued as part of a reduced salary scheme that allowed me to work for four years and then take the fifth year off.

I had always planned to have that year off. And when the time came, it was exactly what I needed. I owed it to myself and my family to make the most of it and do everything in my power to ensure that I would never again unravel to the extent that I did in February 2013.

I have always loved to walk. As a child growing up I used to spend many solitary, happy hours roaming the countryside near where we lived. On holiday I would walk for hours on some of Ireland's magnificent sandy beaches, lost in imagination and thought. My parents were great ramblers. I think they probably covered just about all of the many beautiful walks that criss-cross the Northern Irish countryside. Later, in their retirement they enjoyed many walking holidays in Europe.

One of my first holidays with Ian was on a walking holiday in the spectacular English Peak District and we spent our honeymoon walking in Scotland. I wouldn't recommend camping in Scotland in August, what with the chilly temperatures and the midges, but the walking I would highly recommend.

In her book, *Thrive*, Arianna Huffington states that walking '… makes us healthier, it enhances cognitive performance, from creativity to planning and scheduling, and it helps us to reconnect with our environment, ourselves, and those around us.' In the maelstrom of my middle years I had lost that connection with the earth and forgotten how good walking in the open air made me feel.

In my rush from home to school to work to school and back home to get through what needed to be done I neglected the simple act of putting one foot in front of another, not to get from A to B, but just because it feels so damn good to be out in the fresh air. I don't need to read the latest research, and there is a lot of it, to understand the healing power of nature, and to know that time spent outside in a natural setting has a huge impact on mental health. And walking is one of the best ways of doing this, particularly a walk where you leave your phone behind and engage fully and mindfully with the sights, smells and textures all around us. Nature gives us the space we need to restore and replenish our spirits.

You don't have to travel overseas to walk in beautiful scenery. I have a renewed appreciation for all the walking that can be done close to home. Along the coast, in the hills, Kings Park, around lakes. It is all there for us to explore. If I can, I'll walk to the shops rather than drive.

But when the opportunity to travel to Spain and walk part of the *Camino de Santiago* presented itself, my spirits soared. I spoke the language and relished the prospect of reconnecting with the country and giving my linguistic skills, as well as my body and spirit, a work out.

Knowing several people who had walked either all or part of the Camino was a bonus. They were only too willing to give advice on what to take. One friend insisted that I borrow her walking poles, despite my reluctance, based on a rather ignorant assumption that being reasonably fit I wouldn't need them. How wrong I was. So much so that I bought my own poles while there and have been using them back here in Australia. Ian makes fun of me and my poles but I love them.

I flew from Perth via Dubai to Barcelona, where Julie was waiting for me with the rest of the group. After an afternoon and evening exploring the laneways and narrow streets of the historic *El Born* district and eating far too many tapas, the short flight to Santiago took us to the beautiful province of Galicia, where we met up with the other two members of our group and our local guide, Sabela, who would be accompanying us throughout the walk.

As well as transporting our luggage, Sabela proved to be a wonderful source of information, giving us invaluable insight into the Camino and its history. She joined us for some meals and never tired of answering our questions or telling another of her many anecdotes and stories about past pilgrims and the towns along the way. While she spoke excellent English, I could converse with Sabela in Spanish when the opportunity arose, which was wonderful. It had been twenty-five years since I'd been in Spain and in rediscovering the language I was connecting with yet another part of myself that had lain dormant for too long.

We drove from Santiago to the village of *O Cebreiro*, the starting point for our walk. As our minibus climbed higher the rain began to fall and the hill top was shrouded in mist. I was enchanted. A simple, rustic inn, owned by the family of the priest who had first marked out the Camino with the now famous yellow arrows, was our home for the first night. We collected our passports in the little church, shared a meal with fellow pilgrims and after a restorative sleep I awoke to the one of most spectacular views I have ever seen.

As I peered through my curtains to see the rising sun illuminating the hills all around with its rays of gentle morning light, and the clouds hanging softly in the valley below, I quite literally thought I had died and gone to heaven.

Walking the *Camino de Santiago* is another thing that is very on trend these days. Every second person in Perth seems to have done all or part of it, or be planning to do it at some stage. I really didn't know much about it and didn't know what to expect, but I had watched the film, *The Way*, with Emilio Estevez and his father Martin Sheen, and James Nesbit and that really annoying Dutch character. Not that I have anything against the Dutch, you understand. I have been to Amsterdam and Rotterdam and visited all the museums and eaten the most amazing Ristafel in Utrecht. So I have no prejudice against the Dutch. But if I'd had to walk with that character on the Camino my serenity and good will to all humankind would have been sorely tested.

I digress, yet again.

My time on the Camino surpassed every possible expectation I might have had if I'd had any expectations, which I didn't. It was spectacular, amazing, awesome, uplifting and every other superlative adjective you could possibly think up. I was in my own little bubble of peace and contentment. I was filled with love for the human race and beginning to also like myself a little bit more every day. I felt connected to the universe and part of something much greater, bigger and better.

For a start, it was spectacularly beautiful and we were blessed with the most wonderful spring weather with a perfect walking temperature of about 25 degrees. The chilly mornings provided a bracing, refreshing and invigorating start to each day and as the sun rose in the sky the glorious Galician landscapes unfolded before us. Rolling hills, leafy glades, shady woods, babbling (yes, babbling) brooks, meadows filled with spring flowers, even an underwater village lying secretly beneath a mysterious lake, charming hamlets, bustling towns, farms and people toiling in the fields. Just the most stunningly perfect landscape. The perfect environment in which to replenish, refresh and restore harmony.

I've said it before and I'll say it again. Lucky, lucky me.

It was while walking on the Camino that I began to grieve properly for my dad and my sister. I shed many tears along the way. My dad had always loved to walk, loved wide open spaces, loved the green of Ireland of which Galicia was so reminiscent. My sister, too. She'd loved to escape into the hills, but despite the obvious connection she had with Nature, she was never able to beat her demons, to conquer her alcoholism, to find the peace I wish she could have known.

I thought about my sister as I walked and I asked her to forgive me for not being a better sibling to her, for not being someone she had felt able to confide in. I had a very intense time by a stream that reminded me of a place we used to go in our childhood. I felt her presence. I really felt her presence. I have no idea if it was real or imagined, but it doesn't really matter. The fact is that I was aware of something much greater than me, of a universe that knows no boundaries, and it was reassuring.

I thought of my dad, of his stoicism and stubbornness and the strict maxims by which he lived his life and I thought that he'd done his best. He'd been a good father in many ways. He'd given me life after all. When he died and I didn't go back for his funeral, I wrote my own eulogy for him and sent it to my Mum. My brother and sister told me they didn't know the man I wrote about. That devastated me at the time and I felt as though they were suggesting I was disingenuous. I was very upset and in the wake of my siblings' comments, I'd forgotten about that eulogy. But there, on the Camino, I remembered the comfort it had brought me to write it and I remembered the reasons why I'd written it. I'd wanted to focus on the positive and express my gratitude for what Dad gave me rather than what he didn't give me.

As well as the grief I was able to finally show, it was on the Camino that I began writing verses in my head, verses for children and for myself, as I tramped along the highways and byways of northern Spain, and continued writing in my journal. Documenting my thoughts, feelings and impressions brought great comfort, a new perspective on life and the occasional flash of insight. At the end of one particular glorious day I wrote the following verse:

Camino

A new day dawns bringing inspiration
Can I make it happen, this transformation?
Stopped by a stream, gentle and cool
Aching feet bathed in a sacred pool.
Gentle Hans with his arm in a sling
Spoke of his life, made my soul sing.
Walked with my friend, spoke for a while
Our hearts united, she makes me smile.
My muscles are aching, my ligaments torn
But my spirit soars, I am reborn.

Chapter 18
FINDING ROOTS

Maybe your country is only a place you make up in your own mind. Something you dream about and sing about. Maybe it's not a place on the map at all, but just a story full of people you meet and places you visit, full of books and films you've been to.
~ **Hugo Hamilton,** *The Speckled People: A Memoir of a Half-Irish Childhood*

Recent events in Europe have caused me to reflect on my identity and where I belong in this world. During a long dinner party one evening while staying with friends in France earlier this year, the conversation flowed as freely as the wine – animated and thought-provoking. We discussed many things: immigration, refugees, racism, politics – the well-informed and passionate type of discussion so relished by the French. At one point, while we were talking about the different places we had lived, I was asked if I felt *déracinée* – uprooted. This caused to me reflect on where I have come from, where I have lived and where I may decide to live in future.

I grew up in Northern Ireland at the height of the troubles in the 1960s and 1970s. While we lived in a relatively peaceful area, I have vivid memories of overturned buses burning in the streets of Belfast, of army check points, of being frisked going into shops, of bomb threats causing school evacuations and, on at least one occasion, of the windows of our house shaking under the impact of a bomb at the factory down the road. It was a divided society. Catholics and Protestants went to different schools and lived in separate communities.

With an English mother and an Irish father who did not buy into the extremism of either side, I was to a large extent sheltered from the bigotry and hatred that were characteristic of the times. While I was aware of the tension, of the strong army presence on the streets, as a child I did not fully understand the conflict; all I knew was that there were bad people and I had recurring nightmares about bad men that might do evil things to me and my family.

Yet despite the political issues and the sectarian violence that pervaded all aspects of our lives, my childhood was by and large a happy one. Ireland, north and south, is stunningly beautiful. The Antrim Coast, the Glens of Antrim, the Mountains of Mourne – no song or poem could ever do justice to the magnificence of the landscape.

In the years since my parents died, I have been trying to make sense of my relationship with them, their legacy to me, to understand who these people were who brought me into the world. We didn't have the close relationship I envy in friends who are able to confide in their mother and/or father, for whom they are more like friends than parents. But when I go back to Ireland, I can feel their presence. They gave me the very best childhood they could, a childhood of brooks and streams, of rocky coves and sweeping beaches, of wild headlands and magical woodlands. They showed me the beauty of the natural world, the splendour all around us to which I increasingly turn when life becomes overwhelming. For that I will always be thankful. That is how I choose to look at my parents now, and, how I will remember them.

By the 1980s all my siblings had moved across to England and in due course I followed, going to university in Leeds. It was a huge change for a shy and innocent girl from a quiet market town. My first uprooting. My new English friends seemed so worldly and sophisticated and, as an eighteen year old, England seemed so much more exciting. I forgot the rolling hills, the peaceful glens and windswept shores and soon adapted to a different way of life, to my new found independence amidst the heady student world of the 1980s.

As a post-graduate I moved to London for a time during the excesses of Thatcher's yuppified Britain – my second uprooting, from the north to the south of England. But underneath all the parties and good times I lacked confidence, was unsure of myself, did not yet know who I was or what I wanted. I made some bad choices, spent time overseas in a doomed and abusive marriage, felt restless and directionless, until, replanted in England, to coin a catchphrase from the comedy show Armstrong and Millar, I became a teacher.

But for me, teaching was not a last resort, it was a vocation and has served me well ever since. Both my parents were teachers, as were two of my grandparents, so it was clearly in my blood and courses through my veins to this day.

Apart from short periods living abroad, England became my home until I moved to Perth in 1999. During the 80s my parents had sold our house and moved across the sea to retire in South Derbyshire. It was a nice enough area, but it was not my family home. While I mourned the loss of our home in the place of my birth, I put down strong roots in each of the places I have called home in England. I have very happy memories of my university years in Leeds. A recent thirty-year reunion was testament to the strength of the bonds, friendships and memories forged while there. When we met for a weekend in Leeds it was quite literally just like yesterday; the years in between seemed to disappear and it blew me away to rejoice in the company of friends I hadn't seen for three decades and feel such an intense connection after all this time.

One of my closest friends from school is now back living in Northern Ireland with her husband, who is from New Zealand (funny how we both married Antipodeans), and I visit when I can. Each time I see Strangford Lough from the air as the plane descends to land amongst the greenest fields you'll ever see, I am transcended. I feel a part of this land, it is in me and of me. The older I get, the stronger I feel this connection to Ireland – a visceral call that makes my soul sing and my spirit soar. This is where I crawled along the sand as a baby, chewing shells. This is where I jumped over the waves holding hands with Dad. This is the coastline I escaped to when I needed time out and wanted to think. These are the lanes and hedges and fields of my youth. They defined me as a child and increasingly define me now. When I am there I feel strong and rooted.

And yet when I return to Perth and sit on the beach at sunset, and gaze out to the passing ships on the horizon, I feel strong and rooted here too. I am looking at the same sun I have always looked at and my childhood by the sea echoes strongly in my life near the sea now. We have built a home here for our children. It will always be their home, and mine too, but I have several. England, Ireland, France, Australia, they are all a part of me and each country adds a different dimension to my life.

CHANGING LIGHTBULBS

I am a citizen of the globe and I love to travel. As I grow older, I hope and expect to spend more time in each country, retracing old footsteps, making new ones, perhaps putting down new roots temporarily – Italy appeals, or Spain again perhaps. There is so much to see, explore and do and time is short. The key is to be present wherever one may be, to enjoy each place for what it is.

Unlike Hugh Mackay, who in his book *The Art of Belonging* questions the benefits of travel, I find that it feeds our curiosity and nurtures our self-awareness. I really enjoy Hugh's books and find him to be an intelligent and insightful social commentator, but on the subject of travel I am not wholly in agreement with him. He acknowledges that it may broaden the mind, but warns that it also creates the thought that this charming little village in Umbria or Tuscany could be just the place for you. Well, I stayed in a couple of charming little villages in Umbria and Tuscany when I travelled around Italy on my own in 2009 and it couldn't have been more perfect for the time I was there. I may not have achieved absolute enlightenment but the beauty of the surroundings, the peace and tranquility found there, most certainly created a renewed state of well-being and harmony.

Hugh warns that there is no wondrous community waiting to embrace us. Of course there isn't, but if you travel with an open mind and a warm heart people are far more often than not welcoming and embracing. I certainly felt very embraced by those little hilltop towns I stayed in, and have since returned to explore other parts of Umbria, Tuscany and the rest of Italy. I find that distance lends a new perspective to problems, while travel brings an openness to new experiences, and new ways of looking at the world that can only be beneficial.

So do I feel *déracinée* after years of travelling and living in both hemispheres? At times I have, I sometimes still do when I see scenes from England's green and pleasant land, or hear an Irish accent, or watch the French news, but I feel very lucky to have several places in this world that I can call home and to have my roots spread far and wide.

Sail away from safe harbour
Catch the trade wind in your sails
Explore, dream, discover.

~ Mark Twain

Chapter 19
FINDING ELLIE

Marley taught me about living each day with unbridled exuberance and joy, about seizing the moment and following your heart. He taught me to appreciate the simple things — a walk in the woods, a fresh snowfall, a nap in a shaft of winter sunlight. And as he grew old and achy, he taught me about optimism in the face of adversity. Mostly, he taught me about friendship and selflessness and, above all else, unwavering loyalty.

~ **John Grogan, Marley and Me: Life and Love With the World's Worst Dog**

I never use to be a dog person. When I was a little girl there was a big black labrador living next door to us and one day, when I was about three, this beast jumped on top of me and knocked me over. Now that I come to think of it, being knocked over by a big black dog seems like a rather chilling portent of what was to happen in 2013 when I fell into the clutches of a metaphorical but much more menacing and scary big black dog.

It wasn't an attack as such, but I was really shaken up, quite bruised, had a few scratches and thereafter developed what can only be described as a phobia of dogs. I was very scared of them. Despite my fear, I often walked home from school, usually on my own, and while I enjoyed the fresh air and the freedom my little heart used to start racing at the sound of a barking dog, or worse still, should I spy a dog in the distance. I became adept at knowing where the dogs were likely to appear and made a point of crossing the street to avoid any unpleasant encounters.

My dog-avoiding adventures happened, of course, decades before the obligatory queue of four wheel drives would begin to form at least half an hour before the end of the school day, so little Tristan or young Alexia doesn't have to walk too far. Determined as I was not to be one of those SUV driving, botox using, perfectly-applied make-up wearing mothers, my children were encouraged to walk home from school from quite an early age. This caused much consternation and not a little nasty gossip amongst the yummy mummies – I was neglectful, I was putting my children at risk, how could I be so irresponsible, and so on and so on. It was about a twenty minute walk from the school to our house. One day I received a phone call from Ben's Year Two teacher (Ben would have been about seven and Daniel about ten) telling me that he was far too young to walk home and that I needed to come and pick him up.

This particular teacher was about half my age and there she was telling me what I should and shouldn't be doing with my children. What is more, she had told Ben this too, thereby giving him completely mixed messages, at an age when most children idolize their teachers and believe that everything they say is true. How dare she, I thought.

Thankfully Ben took it with a grain of salt and was quite happy to keep walking home with Daniel. Two little boys with their back-packs and floppy hats, often holding hands, trotting along happily together, looking at the flowers and the trees and the birds and the butterflies. To this day my boys love to walk and think nothing of a fifteen kilometre hike through the bush or on some remote European hillside.

When Ben went on his first school camp he was really excited and looking forward to doing a 'hike,' which turned out to be no more than about five hundred metres. What a complete disappointment. He'd been expecting at least a two-hour trek through the countryside with minimal rations and wild beasts to contend with. Schools have a lot to answer for with all their rules and regulations and complete mollycoddling of children. Children need adventure and yes, a bit of risk. I'm from the school of parenting that says 'Go off and have an adventure, take some risks.'

On another occasion I was asked to go to the Principal's office. Ben had been caught climbing a tree during recess. Well, you'd think he'd been extorting money from the other children and demanding they give him the treats from their lunch boxes, or beating up the Year Ones in the toilets. Climbing a tree was seen as a heinous crime, a complete breach of school policy and what was I going to do about it?

I found this particular principal rather intimidating. He was a big man with a loud voice, who enjoyed making sweeping mission statements and grandiose speeches, and he made his displeasure very clear. Being the shy and unassertive person that I am I was unable to express my outrage in the face of his criticism of my parenting. What I should have said was that tree climbing needs to be encouraged, all children should be able to climb trees, that some of my happiest childhood memories were of sitting on a branch at the top of my favourite tree in the little wood at the end of my road.

Daniel had been roped in to help get Ben down and it seemed he was also in trouble. Go figure. The upshot of it all was that Ben didn't give a hoot, and Daniel was mortified and worried that his reputation was ruined. At the age of ten for God's sake. Daniel prided himself on being 'good,' on never having been made to sit on the infamous blue chairs outside the Principal's office, and now he feared he would never make house captain and that his copy book was well and truly and irreversibly blotted. Hey, teacher, leave those kids alone.

Anyway, getting back to my terror of dogs. It lasted for most of my childhood, until one holiday when we stayed with some remote cousin of my father's in the Lake District for a few days. I would have been about fourteen by then. Cousin Freddie had a sheep dog called Sally. Maybe the fact that I wanted, at that time, to be called Sally instead of Susan had something to do with the bond we developed. I spent the next week taking her for walks in the park, throwing sticks and balls for her to chase. I just loved that dog. And then of course I wanted my own dog. But my parents were completely against any kind of pets – they take up too much time, they said, they cost a lot of money, they said.

Eventually they allowed me to get a hamster, but it just wasn't the same. I hated the fact that it had to live in a cage and insisted on letting my hamster, Jenny, run around the garden. Of course the inevitable happened and Jenny ran off under the hedge one day never to be seen again. She probably got eaten by the big black dog next door, of whom I was by then less frightened but still wary. I was distraught. So they bought me another hamster, who I named Penny, but I wasn't allowed to take her outside. Hamsters don't have a very long life-span so, inevitably, I found Penny dead in her cage one day. Once again, I was distraught. I was responsible for the death of not one but two hamsters, which pretty much ensured that I would never ever be a dog owner if I wasn't capable of looking after a small rodent.

Determined to make up for my neglectful ways, one early autumn day I found a hedgehog by the side of the road – I think he'd heard the noise of the harvester in the field and scurried away under the hedgerow. He was shaking and seemed afraid. I took him home, to the horror of my parents – 'hedgehogs are full of fleas, Susan' – and looked after him for a couple of weeks. I called him Fred and made him a little enclosure in the living room so he could run around and fed him with bread and warm milk. On the insistence of my parents I released Fred back into the wild when harvesting was complete. And that was the end of my pet ownership experiences as a child. Two dead hamsters and a hedgehog called Fred.

I became more interested in boys than dogs after that, but also discovered over the ensuing years that I had an allergy to dog hair. Why I hadn't been allergic to Sally the sheep dog I'll never know, but thereafter, anytime I came within ten metres of a dog my eyes would start to water, my skin would itch and my throat would constrict to the point where I could barely breathe.

Asthma, ezcema and allergies in general run in our family. I used to suffer terribly from hayfever. There was always a period at the beginning of summer when my eyes were permanently red puffy and swollen from my reaction to all the pollens in the air. So I totally lost interest in dogs again, and did all I could to stay away from them. Dogs and horses. I used to love horses. I envied the girls at school who had their own ponies and went riding at the weekend. I used to bounce around our back garden on my orange Spacehopper – remember those? – pretending I was showjumping. I'd set up a series of jumps and go through the circuit of jumps I'd set up for myself again and again and again. Hours of fun, lost in my imagination.

When I finally got to ride a real horse, I lasted about five minutes before the allergies hit – eyes, nose, breathing, itchy skin, everything. I had to get off pronto. Years later, while on a camping holiday in France, Ian and I we were staying near some stables that were open to the public. My childhood fantasy of cantering across the countryside, hair streaming behind me, moving perfectly in time with the sleek body of the beast between my thighs, returned. We set off, and sure enough, after about five minutes I was screaming, "get me off this fucking horse!"

I couldn't breathe. I got back to the tent and had to dose myself up with antihistamines, take about a hundred frenetic puffs of my ventolin and sleep all afternoon before the reaction subsided. Hideous.

Fast forward several decades. Since the day his class had to talk about their pets and Ben had no pet to talk about, he had wanted to get a dog. On another occasion he came home from school and burst into big ploppy tears. It had been 'bring your pet to school day' and he'd been the only one not to have a pet to show off. He was so sad. "I just want to have something to look after," he said.

He was a really caring child who'd always been very kind to animals and had always loved babies. He went through a phase of really wanting a baby sister so he could help to look after her. I think it might have been something to do with the fact that Ben went to Kindy in the girls' school where I then worked. They took a few boys for a while to boost numbers and Ben spent two very happy years there. The teachers were absolutely fantastic – I take my hat off to anyone who teaches children under the age of five – they do an amazing job – and Ben thrived in the warm and nurturing environment.

Unfortunately for him, we didn't provide the much wanted baby sister. Ian and I both agreed that we were more than happy with our two boys. We were blessed. They were happy and healthy, and as an added bonus they genuinely got on really well despite being very different, and we'd never had to contend with the destructive type of sibling rivalry that plagues many families, my own included.

We loved our little family of four. But I was concerned about Ben's fervent desire to have a dog. It seemed very genuine, more than just a whim, and I felt bad that we weren't able to make his dream come true. In the meantime, my dog phobia had returned after a few unsavoury incidents with irresponsible dog owners whose out of control pets always seemed to make a beeline for me.

Once, when I was out jogging, a dog jumped up and bit me on the shoulder. I was so shocked, I couldn't speak. When I managed to blurt something out and suggested that the animal ought to be put down if he couldn't be kept under control, the owner was unrepentant. No apology, just an 'oh he didn't mean to hurt you' type of reaction. Unbelievable. I realised with hindsight that I should have found out the dog owner's details and reported the incident to the local ranger but at the time, with blood pouring down my arm, I was too stunned to take action. And the owner was as aggressive as her dog, showering me with some choice language when I questioned her dog's right to be on this earth.

It's not the dogs that are the problem, it's the dog owners. Expecting everyone else to love their dogs like they do, even if they jump all over people and bite them. So I henceforth reverted to the fear of dogs I had experienced as a three year old, and whenever I saw one anywhere near me I would cross the road to avoid them.

They say dogs smell fear and in my case that certainly seems to be true. They seemed to hunt me down, determined to terrorise me with their snarling and yapping. After the biting incident, dogs and dog owners became the enemy. I would march up to people on the beach and point out the dogs prohibited signs to them. I would ask people in the park to please keep their dogs under control. And one day, to my shame, I even screamed at one startled lady to "keep your fucking dog away from me" as it ran towards me. All I needed to do was spy a dog in the distance and my heart would start to pound, my chest would constrict and I'd break out in a cold sweat.

Fortunately for Ben, Ian's parents had a dog – quite a nice one actually, although I was very wary of him – and Ben was able to spend a lot of time with Leo while he was growing up, which compensated to some extent for our dog-free house. As Ben got older he became very understanding about my phobia and allergies and realised that it wouldn't be pleasant for me to be exposed to dog hairs, and no more big ploppy tears were shed as he moved out of childhood and into early adolescence.

My thoughts about dog ownership began to change when our neighbours acquired a very cute little cavoodle puppy. I had heard about the burgeoning popularity of –oodle dogs. Anything crossed with a poodle that is – groodle, spoodle, labradoodle – anything goes really. Hopefully the poor old poodles don't mind having to shag all manner of mutts and dilute the purity of their gene pool.

True to the claims, I wasn't allergic to Bella, the cavoodle next door. I couldn't believe it. And she was so very cute that it would have been ridiculous for me to be scared of her. I would rub my face in her coat day after day just to make sure, waiting for the itchy skin and the streaming eyes, but it never happened. Not one wheeze, not even a sniffle, not the remotest urge to scratch. I began to see that it was actually quite nice to have a little dog in the house, a very well behaved and under control one of course, and we began to investigate getting a cavoodle for Ben.

It took a while but in the end we found one. She arrived in our house while I was in England visiting my parents. It was during the time when my dad was very ill in hospital and my mum had been fighting a battle with cancer that was temporarily in remission. It was a tense time. For the first week I stayed on my own in my brother's house as he and my sister-in-law were overseas and made the most of the opportunity to spend time with Mum and Dad on my own. But when my brother and sister-in-law returned the whole atmosphere changed.

I was aware of a huge amount of judgement for not having been there all year while Mum and Dad were both deteriorating. Instead of talking things through calmly, feelings were expressed through anger and sharp words and stomping round the kitchen and just a general unfriendliness and frostiness that matched the bleak winter weather outside. At best it was awkward and at worst it was openly hostile. I am not laying any blame here. It is just the way things were at the time.

I felt very lonely and couldn't talk to anyone about how upset, guilty, anxious, stressed and alone I was feeling, as I felt it would seem selfish given the state of my parent's health. It was around this time that I developed sleeping problems. I had no problem getting to sleep but would usually wake up after an hour or two and spend the rest of the night tossing and turning, rehashing the events and words of the day and wondering how the hell I was going to get through the next twenty-four hours.

When I returned to Australia just in time for Christmas I was exhausted, and when, one week later, my father passed away, I didn't feel up to the journey back for the funeral. Again, layer upon layer of guilt descended on me. I'd been to see my GP when I got home as I wasn't feeling at all well, and he told me in no uncertain terms not to travel back again so soon.

In the middle of all this, Ian and Ben went to pick up our new puppy. While I'd been in England, they went to see some new-born cavoodles and Ben had picked her out of the litter, but we'd then had to wait another six weeks before she was ready to come to her new home.

I remember very clearly the day Ben came into the house cradling her in his arms with such love and care – it was a beautiful sight. Finally he had the dog he'd been wanting for so long. And he was brilliant with her. He did all the toilet training and caring for her in those early weeks when it is a bit like having a new born baby in the house. Me, on the other hand, although I could see how sweet Ellie was, I just couldn't connect with her and it seemed like such a lot of hard work and such a big responsibility to have this new life in our house.

I retreated to the South West on my own for a while and tried to come to terms with my grief, and all the other torrent of emotions I was feeling. I was still exhausted. And then one day the phone rang and I found out that a former colleague had taken her own life. The shock and sadness was immense and when I went back to work for the start of the new school year everything had changed, life seemed interminably bleak and that was when I literally and very publicly fell apart.

So there I was in the house on my own quietly having a complete breakdown with this little puppy wondering who the hell this madwoman was and why she'd had the misfortune to be chosen by such a family. I couldn't respond to her and didn't have the energy to play with her or walk her – not so much post-natal but post-puppy blues – but then I had no interest in doing anything at all except cry and lie on the sofa mindlessly watching episode after episode of Rick fucking Stein's Spanish or Italian or Asian fucking odyssey until I couldn't stand it any more. Piss off Rick, I'd think, with your smug face and your oh so lyrical take on food and culture and life in general.

Actually I quite like Rick Stein, and I probably didn't think that at all, I probably just watched the TV with my glazed eyes and fogged up brain and had no reaction whatsoever.

Having a dog just seemed like one more thing that I couldn't deal with. Ellie would look at me with her big brown puppy dog eyes, daring me to love her, and I would turn away. That's how awful I felt. I couldn't respond to the cutest puppy ever. Ellie is very, very pretty. People always want to stop and pat her and children adore her. But me, cold-hearted me, I spurned her pleading and whining and attempts to break through my fog of despair.

And then one day Ian told me that it was my turn to walk her. Turns? We didn't have turns. There was no dog walking roster that I knew of. She was Ben's dog and he did all the walking. But Ian insisted. So very reluctantly off I went one morning with little Ellie on the end of a very long lead and put one foot in front of the other. That was a huge thing for me, just to get out of the house. And gradually, very gradually, Ellie broke through my wall, broke down my defences and found her way into my heart. I fell in love with her. I owe her such a lot. Even on my worst days I would somehow find it in me to walk her, all through the winter, through the wind and the rain, my walks with Ellie kept me going and became an integral part of my recovery.

Four years later I still love her to bits and I spoil her more than anyone else in our house. She is supposed to have her own chair but is often to be found curled up on the sofa with me, much to Ian and Ben's amusement. They still remind me that I am the "Get your fucking dog away from me" crazy lady and they think it is hilariously funny that not only am I absolutely besotted with Ellie but that I now love meeting and talking with other dog owners on my regular walks. They think it is so damn funny. And it is. It really is. It has been a complete turn around.

And other people who knew I didn't like dogs have also been quite amused, "I never thought I'd see you with a dog, Sue," they say with disbelief. There is a big lesson in all of this. If we open up our minds and hearts, we can change, we can grow and develop and find new directions and do things we never thought possible.

As well as finally getting what dogs are all about, the joy of the unconditional love they provide and the special bond we have, it was with Ellie by my side that I rediscovered the beauty of the natural world and tapped into the healing power of nature on our many walks through the bush and on the beach and in parks and around lakes. It gave me a whole new appreciation of how much beauty there is so close to home. I owe a lot to Ellie. Most certainly my sanity and quite possibly my life.

"Happiness is a warm puppy."
~ *Charles M. Schulz*

Chapter 20
FINDING WORDS

In the end, it was the secrets that held me hostage and fuelled my depression, but, once released, emancipation – from fear, shame, guilt and judgement – was finally possible.
~ **B.G. Bowers**, *Death and Life*

While I was growing up I was never encouraged to speak up or speak out. In fact, it was the opposite. I listened and learned but I rarely said very much at all. It was all in my head. One benefit of this is that I am a really, really good listener. An excellent listener. And that's a rare skill I find. There are so many people just desperate to hear the sound of their own voices, who never fully engage in conversation, who speak at you and not with you, who look over your shoulder to see if someone more interesting is there, or who nod furiously while you are speaking while waiting for the opportunity to start talking again themselves, without processing your words. The world needs more listeners. It is, however, important to be able to express oneself and that is not something that comes easily to me.

In the aftermath of my depression, I contracted into myself for a long time. I felt silenced by shame and stigma. I felt humiliated and diminished. No-one encouraged me to speak up and share my experiences. So I just shut up. I shut the fuck up. And it nearly drove me crazy.

There was so much going on in my head and it just had to come out. And then one day I remembered that I'd called the *beyondblue* helpline during a particularly hellish week when I was wrestling with whether or not to resign from my job, and I had a look at their website. There was a forum for sharing your experiences and I did just that. I wrote everything down and it felt amazing. I then saw that they were looking for more people to join their Ambassador and Speaker bureau to help raise awareness about mental health.

I'd heard about *beyondblue* through school and through the media. I thought that to be an Ambassador you had to be well known and have a celebrity profile, like Jessica Rowe or Johanna Griggs. I couldn't imagine that anyone would be interested in listening to little old me. It's such a good thing that more and more celebrities, sports men and women, and people in the public eye are speaking up about mental health. Perhaps it's easier to do with a public profile. You have an automatic platform to reach people, you are well known and recognisable so in some ways you have found your way into people's hearts so there is less fear of being judged.

I don't know. I do think that it may be harder for ordinary people like me to speak out – we need to keep our jobs and feed our families and face our friends. There may just be more stigma amongst the general public than in the celebrity world. I'm not sure. Anyway, I submitted an application, which led to a telephone interview, which in turn led to my attendance at a training day, and now I am very proud to be a part of this growing voluntary nationwide community working to raise awareness about depression and anxiety, reduce stigma and increase understanding. And it is just the best thing ever.

When I started, I really didn't know what to expect. Despite my innate shyness I am pretty comfortable standing up and speaking in public. I always prepare really thoroughly, and know exactly what I am going to say. I do use my notes, although I'd like to get to the point where I can speak without them.

Throughout my teaching career there have been quite a few occasions when I've had to stand up and address large groups – sometimes just students, but also parents, other teachers and the school governors. I really enjoy crafting a speech. On one occasion, a photographer who was covering a valedictory event at the end of the school year came up to me and told me he'd never been so affected by a speech before – he'd heard me the previous week at another occasion, where I'd attempted to be funny and it had gone down very well. He told me I had a special gift to be able to make people laugh one minute and then cry the next. I kind of shrugged off his compliments at the time but he may just have been right.

Self-belief, as you have probably gathered, is not my forte. But I am beginning to believe in my speaking abilities just a little bit more as each time I've done a *beyondblue* event I've had such heartfelt, warm and uplifting feedback. It makes my heart sing to stand up and reach out to people.

I remember my first event. It was on a ship. The navy had been making mental health a focus in the lead up to Christmas and had also done a fund-raising exercise. I was invited to receive the cheque on behalf of *beyondblue* and to give a short presentation. I remember looking at the sea of uniforms facing me as I stood on the bridge of the ship and addressed the sailors. It felt so right, as if I'd always been meant to be there, standing on the ship with the sea all around on a windy day in the early summer. Everyone was so respectful and thankful and appreciative. I was blown away. Not literally, as I would have ended up in the sea, but I was just thrilled.

So beginning to find my voice and being able to share my experiences and maybe even have an impact and help others is just one of the many positive things that have come out of my depression and anxiety. 'Authentic' is a bit of a buzz word at the moment, and I'm always wary of buzz words and trends, particularly in the whole well-being industry, but since I've been speaking about my experiences I feel so much more authentic, much more like myself. I just wish I hadn't waited so long to discover this new improved version of myself. But maybe this is just how is was meant to be.

That's another cliché isn't it, along with 'everything happens for a reason.' It was meant to be. Well I don't know about that, but what I do know is that only when we accept how things are, and find the positive in a bad situation, do we have the capacity to do some good in the world and thrive again. I was determined to create something meaningful out of my experiences, and so far it seems to be happening.

Sue came to speak about her journey through anxiety and depression at our annual conference in September 2016. A lot of our delegates went to talk to Sue after the presentation, as she was very approachable and really humanised the feelings ... we were grateful for her time and her willingness to share her story with so many people. It really resonated with our delegates and reminded them of why they do the work they do. Sue was very personable. With humour and a clear flow her words managed to hit home really well.

~ **Natasha, Red Cross Delegate**

Chapter 21

FINDING CHILDHOOD

*If you carry your childhood with you,
you never become older.*

~ **Tom Stoppard**

Well Tom, my body is definitely getting older, but I have been learning how to feel more youthful and vibrant and less inhibited in my mind. One of the best ways to do this is to remember how you felt and what you loved to do as a child.

Take television. The screens that surround and accompany us everywhere we go today bear very little, if any, resemblance to the television set that sat proudly in the corner of our living room in the 60s and 70s. Being reactionaries rather than radicals, my parents were always a few steps behind everyone else in society when it came to gadgets, devices and electrical appliances. Well more like half a century behind in actual fact.

I have vivid memories of my mother washing everything by hand at the kitchen sink – no such thing as a laundry in our modest 1960s bungalow – scrubbing away with a huge cake of green soap and a wash board to remove the most stubborn of stains. We had a mangle close to the back door through which clothes were wrung numerous times before being hung on the washing line, which was suspended diagonally across our back garden, supported in the middle by a hefty wooden prop. No Hills Hoist for us, no compact, more practical use of space, no thank you very much.

My mother had some bizarre notion that the clothes wouldn't dry as well if they were hung close together on a circular contraption. So the washing line remained. It did come in very handy as a badminton net, I have to say, so it wasn't all bad. Not until I was a teenager did we get our first washing machine, a twin tub of which my mother was inordinately proud, but which took up rather a lot of space in our kitchen and which shook, trembled and made an alarmingly loud and unpleasant noise that drowned out all conversation when in spin cycle.

I have mostly hazy, but occasionally vivid memories of time spent with my mother as a very young child listening to the radio, or watching television. The aptly named *Listen with Mother* and *Watch with Mother* would provide fifteen minutes or so of entertainment for us each day. While the use of 'mother' in the title of these programmes may seem rather quaint and old-fashioned, there was something magical and very special about sitting down together to watch or listen. Television wasn't then just a babysitting device. It was something to be shared and talked about afterwards. We loved *The Flower Pot Men, Tales of the Riverbank, Andy Pandy* and *Camberwick Green*. You can see all of these programmes now through the wonders of YouTube. They seem so calm, peaceful and serene, relics from a bygone era when children still climbed trees and played in the street.

I adored television. My favourite shows captured my imagination and transported me to magical lands and far away places where I could forget, for a while, my shyness and sense of somehow not fully belonging. I loved watching cartoons like *Top Cat* and *Marine Boy* and *Scooby Doo* and *Noggin the Nog*. There were others like *Shazzam*, where magic happened when two halves of the same ring connected, and *Journey to the Centre of the Earth*.

I loved everything to do with magic and adventure and anything that involved travelling to distant horizons, escaping the mundane and the everyday. I remember rushing to finish my homework on a Monday night so that I could follow the adventures of Hannibal Hayes and Kid Curry, two cowboys permanently on the run from the law in the series *Alias Smith and Jones* starring the rather easy on the eye Ben Murphy who I think was my first real crush.

We loved *Star Trek* and *Dr Who*, although my brother used to delight in scaring me with his imitations of the monsters and creatures. Then there were those iconic American series, *Dallas* and *Dynasty* – I was more of a *Dallas* girl myself – can still here the title music in my head, and very English drama like *Upstairs Downstairs*, *The Pallisers* and *Poldark*, which became my *Watch with Mother* through my teens.

We didn't have a colour television until I was fourteen. I remember the day we finally got one, at least five years after everyone else. It was December, and I had to leave to sing in a Christmas carol concert when it arrived. I was desperate to watch it and could barely contain my excitement. I raced home after the concert and spent the rest of the night having my first colour television experience. I remember it as if it were yesterday. I remember what I was wearing, and how I was sitting, my back against the radiator, my legs stretched out in front of me.

I watched the film *Carousel*. I have never forgotten that moment. The colours on the screen seemed so alive, so magical, so amazing to me, and my love of television remains to this day. Now we have television on tap – twenty-four hours a day, seven days a week – wherever and whenever we want. We are drowning in television. We have Netflix and Foxtel – although it is amazing how often there really is nothing on worth watching – and iview and catch up TV. We can binge watch to our heart's content. I'm not so sure it is a good thing.

There was something wonderful about having to wait a whole week to find out what would happen next. Something about delayed gratification that today's youth know so little about. (God, how old do I sound?) It made watching the next episode in a series something to be anticipated, savoured, remembered, not something to be taken for granted. I knew the times of all my favourite programmes and scheduled my homework accordingly. Not that I watched television for very many hours a day. It would have been one hour a day at the very most, which made it even more special.

When I was depressed I watched a lot of television without really taking anything in or caring about what happened to any of the characters. For someone who couldn't wait to find out who shot JR, this was a very sorry state of affairs. It was just a background of noise and images I used to drown out the chaos going on in my head.

But now I'm back in full TV watching and appreciating mode, and have been for quite some time. Far too much for Ian's liking. He hates reality TV, while it is one of my guilty pleasures. I don't love them all, but I really enjoy the psychology and mind games of shows like *Survivor*, and watching how all those beautiful people interact and bitch and jostle for position on the *Bachelor* and *Bachelorette* – although those recent series of the latter have really not been up to scratch. I don't mind a good cooking show either, and for a while I was obsessed with property shows, particularly Phil and Kirsty, although I think they have now well and truly peaked.

It is very easy to waste hours mindlessly watching whatever happens to be on at the time, but I really do enjoy watching a good show on TV. Particularly those that make me cry and laugh, or inspire me to become a better person and to make the most of my modest talents. I think it is a wonderful thing. The same with films. They take me to another place, sometimes to another time. I love true stories, made-up stories, anything that moves and uplifts. I want to laugh and cry, I want to really feel and engage when I watch something, not just watch with cynical detachment.

I love all those back stories the contestants have on *So You Think You Can Dance*, or singing shows like *The Voice*. I love to hear about people's journeys, how they got to where they are, the obstacles they have had to overcome, to hear about what motivates them. Ian just laughs at me. I sometimes get very cross when others don't have the same emotional reaction as I do to something. I want to share that emotion.

We recently started watching a film together as a family on a Friday night and Ian's choice one week was *The Imitation Game*. When it finished I couldn't stop sobbing because I was so moved. It was such a tragic story and I'd had no idea about the ending, I didn't know that he would take his own life. I was devastated.

It's the same with music. I'm with Bob Geldof who I heard describe the way in which a beautiful piece of music moves him to tears. A life without music doesn't bear thinking about. It is the soundtrack of my life. I can remember the songs that were playing in the background at key moments in my youth. I am very thankful for the piano and clarinet lessons my parents signed me up for. We all learnt to play instruments – thanks Mum and Dad. My brother played the violin, and my sister Lesley the piano and later the clarinet like me. Lesley and I were reasonably accomplished – she much more than me on piano and she continues to play in her church – and often performed solos in school concerts.

I think my parents had an overinflated idea of my ability though, and would have liked me to pursue music much further. I enjoyed playing in bands and orchestras and singing in choirs, but I wasn't a natural player and I couldn't really improvise. I had to practise a lot to reach the level I did, and that was not anything particularly special. But I have a good ear for melody, and I can hold a tune.

Music did give me a lot of pleasure as a child, and was another outlet for my shyness. When I played I'd be transported to a more confident version of myself. Mastering a skill is immensely rewarding. Being able to play at least one instrument is something I think every child should do, as well as learning a language. It is good for the brain, it stimulates creativity and enhances fine motor skills and much much more.

While we did share a love of music, my parents and I did not share a taste in music. My father believed the 1960s were responsible for all that was wrong in society. With the 60s came that dreadful pop music don't you know, and all the drugs and sex and promiscuity and the moral abyss that accompanied this iconic decade.

I remember the very first vinyl single I listened to. It was *Be My Baby* by the Ronettes. I listened to it over and over and over again. We also had one solitary Beatles's single – *She*

Loves You. I don't know how these records came to be in our house as my parents seemed to think all pop music was the work of the devil, but there they were to feed my still childish mind with thoughts of love and yearning and dreams of one day finding my knight on a white charger.

Through my teenage years I moved on to ABBA, then the edgier Blondie, and then the Police and the whole punk era that spanned my school and early university years with its clanging and banging and the existential soundtrack to which those disenchanted with Thatcher's Britain clung for meaning and release.

Music and television aside, my childhood was full of nature. Playing all afternoon by streams, building dams, creating dens, tramping across fields, through leafy woodlands and dense forests, quiet valleys and rugged coastlines. Often on my own. I spent hours and hours lost in my own imaginative world where I could be whomever I chose to be.

I loved riding my bike too, speeding down hills as fast as I could the wind in my hair (no helmets in those days), my hands off the handle bars when my balance was perfected. As adult bike riders we seem to have to have a purpose such as some kind of a charity ride, or a weekly lycra clad group trek out to the hills or along the coast, which are all fantastic of course. But I used to jump on my bike and ride simply to feel the air around me and and relish the speed and the sense of freedom and movement and the joy of just being out there peddling, moving.

Sometimes I long to jump on my bike and peddle around the area where I live without a helmet, whizzing down hills with merry abandon, but I would probably get a few strange looks, not to mention a fine for the terrible crime of not wearing a helmet. Don't get me wrong, helmets can and do save lives, but to treat non-helmet wearers like criminals smacks a bit too much of an increasingly controlling nanny society in my book.

We need to embrace the joy of being active for its own sake, not to burn calories or tone muscles but because it just feels so damn good to be out and about and moving our bodies through space and time.

Rollercoasters – love those too – went on some very scary rides at Alton Towers in the UK a couple of years ago. Playing games – we do that lots in our household still. Board games, card games, party games – love them all. We need to be more playful, to do things because they are simply fun. We are so programmed to achieve 'outcomes' in everything we do, whether at work or in our leisure time, to burn those calories or reach that goal. Stop, I want to scream, stop striving for a while and just be, just feel, just live in the moment.

Sweet childish days, that were as long
As twenty days are now.
~ **William Wordsworth**, *To a Butterfly*

Chapter 22
FINDING KNOWLEDGE

We read to know we're not alone.
~ **William Nicholson**, *Shadowlands*

When I was depressed I couldn't focus for long enough to read for any length of time. I'd find myself just staring at the same page trying to make sense of the words. I could see them, but they weren't connecting with my brain. It was beyond distressing. I have a lifelong love of reading and I always had my head in a book as a child. So not being able to read was like having a vital organ removed or an arm cut off.

I never go on holiday without a whole pile of books to read – real books, not the electronic version, so my suitcase often exceeds the weight limit, or I end up with one pair of shoes to reduce my load. Books, I cannot do without. I cannot bear to have nothing to read.

The temporary severing of my mind from the wonderful world of literature only served to increase my despair. I felt that I could deal with anything as long as I had a book to read. But my mind had shut down, my brain was betraying me, depriving me of something that is almost as important to me as water or air.

When I was a little girl I received a book as a school prize. It was called *My Big Book of Geography*. I was five. This book was a wonder to me. As I gazed at the bright, colourful pages I was transported to foreign lands filled with unfamiliar sights and different-looking people. I marvelled at the vivid pictures; I still have this book and it still stirs the same wonder in me.

Today, we can trawl the Internet and have images of the world at our fingertips, but never underestimate the beauty of a book. How amazing, I thought, to be able to visit these places one day and talk to their inhabitants. Books have always stoked my sense of curiosity and stirred feelings of wonder and magic and yearning for faraway places and new experiences. My parents fed this love of the printed word. They read to me every night until I was old enough to read for myself, and even then they would read to me now and again when I was sick or just because I asked them to.

As I write this, I'm having an epiphany. I've written so much about what my parents didn't do, but not enough about what they did do. They introduced me to the world of my imagination, a place I've always been able to go to in times of trial and trouble and sadness and despair. But with depression, that world was taken from me for a while. So when I rediscovered it, I read with a new found fervour as if I was reading for the very first time.

Throughout childhood, I devoured books. I'd read a book a day. I loved all of the Enid Blyton books, anything to do with adventure and exploration. I remember sitting in the car on the way to school with my nose in *Anne of Green Gables* and Mum having to literally prise the book from my hands, so reluctant was I to leave the world of Anne and Gilbert and Marilla and Rachel Lynde, of Avonlea and the Avenue and the Lady of Shalott.

As I began to recover I started to read widely about mental health, accessing articles online, and in books such as *Flourish* by the wonderful Martin Seligman, *Thrive* by Arianna Huffington or the transcendant *Forgiveness and Other Acts of Love* by Stephanie Dowrick, a gently yet intensely powerful work about love and healing and everything that is good about the human spirit. I read accounts of people's journeys with the black dog, books by Stephen Fry and Ruby Wax, a fabulous book called *Overwhelmed* by Brigid Shulte, and the marvellous *Quiet* by Susan Cain.

Discovering what it was I had actually experienced made me feel a whole lot better, and being informed helped me to understand what had happened. Oh my goodness, I thought, I'm not a freak, I shouldn't feel ashamed, there is no need for me to feel guilty, there are so very many people who are just like me.

Books gave me knowledge, and knowledge gave me the power to transform the way I approach life, to change my thought processes. Books were there for me on my path out of the darkness and into the most glorious blaze of light. Books make me laugh and cry and feel. I don't understand people who don't like to read. It breaks my heart when children say they have never read a book, or they'd much rather play computer games. How sad to be deprived of the wonder of words and sentences and chapters and paragraphs, of beginnings and endings.

I am very mistrustful of houses that have no books on display and I refuse to part with any of my own books. Ian recently boxed up some of my old French books. "NO!" I cried, "you can't do that."

"But you never read them," he said.

"No, but they are there, I need to know they are there, they are my friends, they comfort me and I love to look at them and remember the joy of reading them, what I was doing at the time, where I was living."

I have enormous reverence for authors. I love going to the Perth Writer's Festival and listening to writers speak of their work. I've heard Elizabeth Gilbert speak twice and oh my goodness I love that woman. She is so articulate and funny and honest and self-deprecating and just so damn talented. I heard Magda Szubanski and Jane Caro speak about the books they had written and their mental health struggles over the years. Inspirational. I spoke to Jane afterwards and as she signed my book I told her I wanted to write but I was scared. She spoke a lot about fear in her talk. She looked me in the eye and said, "just do it, take a risk."

Gosh, I thought, maybe I will, maybe I could, maybe I should. I took my wonderful mother-in-law to a morning tea with Liane Moriarty at the Hilton in Perth. I was reading Liane's books long before she was popular in Australia might I say, long before *Big Little Lies*, which is the book I would love to have written. I know all the people in that book, those Junior School Mums, I know them all. I spoke to Liane too. She signed the pile of her books I had brought with me, we had a little chat and I was so very inspired.

We need that in life. We need to feel a little awe and a little admiration. I went to see Tim Winton speak a couple of weeks ago and what a wonderful man he is. He spoke more about his philosophies on life than about his latest book – no shameless self-promotion for our very own Tim, just honest insight and authenticity and humility and joy. I love his sense of wonder at the natural world, his belief that, in the words of William Blake 'all that lives is holy,' and that the older he gets the more amazing the natural world seems. Thank you, Tim. Thank you for the way in which you articulate what so many of us feel but which only you can express in your inimitable way.

While I love classic literature, I'm not particular highbrow in my literary tastes these days. I want to be entertained, to be moved, to laugh and cry when I read a book. Ian is a much more esoteric reader than I am. I love the gentle prose of Alexander McCall Smith, which Ian scorns as being about nothing much at all; in many ways that is the point and the very charm of his work. I'm a big fan of JoJo Moyes; *The One Plus One* and *Me Before You* are two of the most intelligent books in their genre I've ever read. Louise Candlish wrote a great book set in Italy about family dynamics and loss that I absolutely loved but I gave it to my niece and can't remember the name. I love crime fiction too, and exploring the workings of the human mind in a good psychological thriller.

Books played a huge part in my recovery, and continue to be an important part of my life. Books encourage us to reach outside of ourselves. There is something deeply spiritual about the impact the imaginatively written word can have. Words and books have the power to make us better than we are, to deepen our knowledge of ourselves and others and the world around us, to expand our insight into the human condition and to uncover universal truths.

> *Books are the quietest and most constant of friends;*
> *they are the most accessible and wisest of counselors,*
> *and the most patient of teachers.*
>
> ~ **Charles William Eliot**

Chapter 23
FINDING FRIENDSHIP

*No person is your friend who demands your silence,
or denies your right to grow.*

~ Alice Walker

As will already be apparent, I have equivocal views on the sisterhood. I have found that as women we are often our own worst enemies, and that any kind of solidarity is sometimes more obvious by its absence than its presence. This makes me sad. At best, the sisterhood is very selective and in my experience Lindsay Lohan and her group of mean girls are alive and well. But things are changing. I am beginning to find my tribe and to understand just how powerful the sisterhood could be if we all pulled together. I have met some amazing women in recent times. If they are reading this, they will know who they are.

I have some very close friends in the UK and in France who I absolutely adore. I don't see them very often, but when we do get together it is as if time has stood still. We pick up where we left off. Time and distance have in no way lessened our bond. In fact, in the last few years, from my point of view, these bonds have become even stronger. I can feel the presence of my friends from 13,000 kilometres away. I miss them hugely and love them all to the moon and back. While he was travelling, I was hugely comforted to know that Daniel was able to stay with some of my friends and I love the fact that our children are now friends in their own right.

Ian and I have stayed in touch with many of our friends from our teaching days in England, and when we meet, often after many years in between, it is just like putting on your favourite T-shirt or most comfortable pair of jeans. It just feels right.

While I was going through my depression I didn't tell a lot of my friends in the UK about what had happened. They didn't have the context, so it wouldn't really have made much sense, and what could they do from the other side of the world? I know, though, that had I reached out they would have been there and listened without prejudice. I have seen many of them since, and we have talked about all or our trials and tribulations over the years. What strikes me each time is that everyone goes through tough times, and we are all united by our common humanity.

This year, when I was back in the UK, I briefly visited some dear friends in the north of England who also happen to be Daniel's godparents. I was with my oldest friend Elizabeth, from school and university days, who is my absolute inspiration in life. I never fail to be uplifted by the grace, dignity and humour with which she bears her MS and the way in which she embraces each day.

We stopped off on the way back from a reunion weekend in Leeds, that wonderful weekend during which old friendships and connections were reignited. As we were talking over lunch, the conversation turned to the last time we'd met, which had been for another reunion, this time of all the past heads of the girls' boarding house where we used to live. Marion made an insightful comment. She said that during that earlier visit "you were there, but not there." She had known instinctively that I hadn't been myself, even though we didn't have a lot of time to spend together. She had been through some tough times herself.

On this occasion, I didn't need to say too much. We understood each other. She expressed her delight in seeing me so happy, and I was simply overwhelmed, as I always am, by the beautiful human beings that both she and her husband Steve are. I love them to bits. I wish they'd come out to Australia, but Marion is a bit daunted by the distance. If you are reading this, Marion, get yourselves a couple of tickets, get on a plane and get out here. You are retired now, you have the time. No more excuses.

I missed all my friends desperately when I first moved to Perth, and found it very difficult to make new ones that would even come close to replacing what I had back in England. At their best female friendships are loving comforting, and nourishing. With true friends we can share our faults, failings, fears and angst without fear of judgement. We can drop the mask we sometimes have to wear when going about our daily business. But friendship can sometimes be disappointing, even destructive. In the words of Steve Irwin, "Crocodiles are easy. They try to kill and eat you. People are harder. Sometimes they pretend to be your friend first."

Throughout my life, I have experienced female friendship in a very intense way. I like to have the time to get to know people really well, to make deep and lasting connections. While at school I had a handful of friends with whom I could share my every thought, each unfolding moment of teenage angst, in minute detail. Some friendships last forever.

Others break your heart. Some take their natural course and end without fuss or drama. Others can have the intensity of a doomed love affair that burns brightly for a while but ultimately implodes. I have had a few friendships like this, friendships that dazzled and beguiled me, only to leave me despondent when I realised that the reality was in fact a mirage that could not last.

I once had a friend who was larger than life. Flamboyant, alluring and much admired. The type of girl who would turn heads as she walked down the street. We connected during some difficult times at work and, for a time, we got on really well. We shared a love of the French language and we just clicked. I made her laugh and she saw me as a bit of a project I think. She decided that I needed a complete wardrobe makeover. She used to say things like "Sue, we need to do something about your shoes." I rarely wear heels. It's comfort every time for me. Life is too short to teeter around in ridiculously high shoes. And I like to walk as much as I can. And I have dodgy ankles and knees. So squeezing my toes into impossible points and lifting my arches to impossible angles is not for me. I like to dress casually and comfortably too.

This friend of mine, however, did not find my casual look appealing and took it upon herself to make me over. It was enormous fun for a while. We'd spend afternoons in boutiques trying everything on. We laughed a lot. I'm not a girly girl, I'm not into hair and make-up and sleek personal grooming. I'm more a scrunch-dry my hair, chuck it up in a just-got-out-of-bed messy kind of way, two-minute make-up, comfy leggings, jeans and coordinating active wear kind of girl. This friend had herself regularly waxed and plucked and tinted and glossed and polished and wouldn't be seen dead in a pair of tracksuit bottoms. She was every beautician's and fashionista's dream, always adorned with the latest accessories, bejewelled with shiny objects, and with the latest Louis Vuitton bag draped casually over her arm. I loved that we were so different and yet got on so well.

I've never mastered the art of carrying a handbag. I always feel encumbered and awkward. I prefer a practical messenger bag or better still, a backpack that leaves my arms free. Spending $2000 on a handbag is not for me. Even if I had the money, I would baulk at the cost. I'd rather buy a plane ticket or treat myself to a few days somewhere lovely.

I loved my friend dearly, I loved her like the younger sister I never had. Sadly, our friendship didn't last. We moved in different circles. She was always out at the latest club or bar, mixing with the in crowd. I like a glass of wine on the sofa with a good movie. On top of that, while we had bonded over difficult times at work, it was work that ultimately drove us apart. I miss the friendship we once had; it burned very brightly for a while and I sometimes wistfully hope that we might be friends again one day.

I know how ephemeral friendship can be, how it can come and go, how we can take up with false friends who only want to use us for their own ends and who will think nothing of betraying our trust for personal or professional gain. But true friendship is kind, patient, accepting, loving and eternal.

Over the past few years I have met some incredible women and made what I hope will become lasting friendships, as well as come to appreciate existing friendships much more. When we came back from Kerala, Julie told me that no matter what time it was, day or night, she would always be there for me at the end of the phone. I have never had to do that, but if I did, I know that she would be true to her word. What a gift friendship is.

In recent years I have made friends through tennis and hockey, through new work connections, with parents from school, neighbours old and new. For someone who often finds group situations difficult, I have several groups of friends now, amongst whom I feel that I can be myself. I have met new people through my travels to Kerala and Spain, through my work with *beyondblue* and through exploring my creative side.

As LM Montgomery says in *Anne of Green Gables*, "Kindred spirits are not so scarce as I used to think. It's splendid to find out there are so many of them in the world."

I now even have friends with whom I mainly communicate through Facebook, which is rather lovely. There is a girl, I'll call her a girl, who I met again at our reunion in Leeds this year. I didn't know her very well at all in the 1980s. She was the partner of another friend of mine; they had met during their year abroad and Jamie used to visit a lot during our final year. I saw her occasionally when we had first left university and a lot of us were living in London, but that was as far as it went.

Now, though, I am friends with this amazing woman I never really knew before. I've discovered that she is not only an accomplished journalist and author, but also a talented songwriter. It's just fabulous. We have also been in email contact and she has been very encouraging about my writing. I hope I'll see her again when we have our next reunion. Meeting her again has encouraged me to trust my creative instincts and to keep writing. Sometimes people come back into your life just when you need them.

Some friends come and go but true friendship lasts a lifetime and is never in question. It transcends long periods apart, separation, deaths, births, marriages, divorces and differences of opinion. Being an introvert does not mean you don't value friendship. Post-depression, I treasure my friends more than ever before, precisely because they allow me to be, and accept me for, who I am. Real friendship means having nothing to prove; it is more about feeling, meaning and connection than about doing.

> *Piglet sidled up to Pooh from behind.*
> *"Pooh!" he whispered.*
> *"Yes, Piglet?"*
> *"Nothing," said Piglet, taking Pooh's paw. "I just wanted to be sure of you."*
> **~ A.A. Milne, *The House at Pooh Corner***

Chapter 24

FINDING NOURISHMENT

*After a good dinner one can forgive anybody,
even one's own relations.*

~ **Oscar Wilde**

I love food. I love the smells, the textures, the colour and the sheer joy of sharing good food and wine with good friends. My ideal day would involve a long, leisurely, lazy lunch somewhere lovely. Perhaps a Tuscan terrace or a Provencal patio or on a gentle south west WA hillside with a sweeping winery vista. Not a fly in sight but the gentle hum of bees somewhere in the background and the rhythmic chirping of cicadas adding to the sleepy summer vibe. A warm summer's day, but not so hot that it is uncomfortable sitting outside. A long table with assorted chairs, not the perfect matching outdoor setting that seems to be de rigueur these days. Checkered table cloths, pichets of white, red and rosé wine, large platters filled with food to share and savour.

I didn't get my love of food from my parents. When we were growing up our familial meals were pretty staple 60s and 70s fare. Overcooked meat and two or three soggy vegetables. My mother wasn't a natural cook by any means. When my parents first married it was my dad who had more idea about domesticity, having lived on his own and supported himself all through university, while my mother, at the ripe old age of nineteen, wasn't much more than a child bride.

I knew no better, and we were well fed and looked after, but even as a child I baulked at some of the concoctions my mother would produce. There was a particularly glutenous macaroni cheese and something called egg pie, which kind of defies description. My favourite was shepherd's pie, which I used to eat with lashings of tomato ketchup, and Mum's chicken and vegetable soup which she always made with fresh stock from the carcass of the Sunday roast. My dad loved to do a fry-up which involved pouring about half an inch of oil into a frying pan and cooking all the meat for well over thirty minutes until it all became a kind of greyish homogeneous mess. The first time I tasted a medium rare sirloin steak was a revelation and bore absolutely no resemblance to the tough and tasteless steaks I had eaten as a child.

My mum did excel at baking – see the aforementioned condom in the apron pocket incident – and there were always freshly-baked biscuits and cakes, which did nothing for my waistline once I had hit puberty and transformed from a skinny kid to a slightly-embarrassed-about-her-curves teenager. And puddings, my parents were good with puddings such as lemon meringue pie and steamed pudding; all those good old fashioned calorie-ridden desserts were done very well in our household.

I remember my mother getting a bit adventurous with those Vesta curries you used to buy in a packet – remember those? We used to think we were really exotic eating Vesta curries. Quite dreadful really with those cubes of reconstituted chicken – apparently it was chicken but who knows, it could have been anything at all. We had little dishes of coconut and raisins and for some strange reason bananas on the side. Not a freshly ground spice or lime pickle in sight. And so I left home with neither much culinary skill nor a highly-developed palate, but as soon as I began to discover the big wide world of gastronomic delights I caught on quickly and now consider myself to be a pretty good cook; I also really, really love to eat.

But when I was depressed, I stopped eating for a while. Not intentionally. I just had no interest whatsoever in what I did or didn't put in my mouth and I couldn't be bothered. For someone who has always loved food and always been just a few kilos more than the recommended weight (it's my bones really, you know, I've always had big bones), this meant something was very wrong with me.

Ian and I used to laugh at that Billy Connolly routine where he makes fun of women who like to say they are retaining water when they are overweight. "You're not retaining water," says Billy, "you're retaining chips."

Ah chips – one of my big weaknesses. I've retained quite a few of them in my life. While not exactly packed with nutritional goodness they taste so damn good, particularly with a cold beer or a chilled SSB. By chips, I mean what the British call crisps, not hot chips. Favourite flavours are the iconic Tayto cheese and onion, only available in Northern Ireland, and which I always have to have when I stay with my friend Elizabeth. My favourite crisps now are Tyrells – I was first introduced to them at my brother's house and was most impressed, so great was my delight one day when, for the first time, I spied some Tyrells chips in my local Coles. We have to be a bit careful about our crisp intake in our household.

So crisps are a big weakness of mine. It's very stressful being married to a man like Ian who carries not an ounce of fat on his body. He is so damn disciplined about what he eats – it drives me crazy. I'd love to see him go nuts one day and devour a packet of TimTams, or eat too much of anything really. And he is so very scathing about fat people. A bit like my dad was. My dad used to think that being fat was a sign of ill-discipline and a slovenly mind. He used to run marathons to burn up all those puddings and fat-rich meals, and did so much exercise he could get away with eating pretty much anything. Despite his scorn for the less honed and toned members of the human race, Ian seems quite accepting of me and my additional five kilos and strangely expanding tummy.

Crisps aside, I generally eat a pretty good diet and enjoy the whole culture and aesthetic of food. I'm not such a fan of the foams and the infusions and the more extreme and precious aspects of modern cuisine, and am mindful that never having to worry about where my next mouthful will come from is a luxury on a planet where too many people don't have enough to eat.

I enjoy watching food programmes on TV although I probably watch less of them now that there is a bit of over-saturation going on. I'm not a fan of the Australian version of *Masterchef* but I do enjoy the British version. I liked Rachel Khoo a lot when she did her *Little Paris Kitchen* and London and Melbourne programmes but now she has gone all Channel Ten so I'm not so sure any more. The previously maligned Rick Stein is always entertaining and articulate. I actually ate in one of his restaurant in 1996 when I was pregnant with Daniel and we were in holiday in Cornwall. Although I remember that my sister-in-law's mother once fell on the steps outside his restaurant and broke her wrist. Apparently, they were not very helpful when it came to claiming the insurance pay out to which she was entitled.

Preparing a beautiful meal for friends and family makes me very happy. I can think of no better way to spend a day, time-allowing of course, than in the kitchen, prepping and creating a culinary feast. Ian and I enjoy eating out, but we tend to save our restaurant-going for the holidays, when we are more relaxed and have the time to taste and savour every morsel.

We love the wineries of the South West, the quality of the restaurants in Melbourne, and, of course, the food in France. There is nothing quite like a French market for colour and smell and texture and the sheer joy of food, and talking about food, although there are also some amazing markets on our own doorstep, and more and more farmers' markets across Australia.

Over the last few years Ian has been honing his bread-making skills to the extent that we very rarely have to buy bread now. When he first came back to England, just before we got married, he baked bread now and again, but now there is no stopping him. Consequently our house is often filled with the aroma of freshly-baked bread, which has done nothing to diminish the size of my tummy but much to feed my soul and my spirit, so delicious are his loaves.

He makes all kinds of bread from scratch, makes his own starter culture for sour dough and being the scientist that he is, approaches the whole process in a logical and methodical manner. I think that in a former life he must have been one of the great bakers of the world. He is that good. But he is so modest about his skills. He is hoping that when we finally move into our renovated house we will be able to incorporate a bread oven so that he can expand his operations and produce enough for others in the community to enjoy.

Good food must be accompanied by good wine. There have been more than a few times through the years when I've overindulged in alcohol, but now I'm much more restrained and discerning in what I drink. I do enjoy a good gin and tonic now and again, and drink both beer and wine, generally in modest amounts. A jug of Pimm's always goes down well on a hot summer's day and I enjoy the nostalgic aspect of this very English drink too.

Given my sister's alcoholism I have always been a bit wary about drinking regularly but I figure that if I was going to be an alcoholic it would have happened by now. When work was particularly stressful, it was very easy to reach for the wine bottle every night just to get a bit of a release, but interestingly, when I was depressed, drinking was the last thing I wanted to do. I felt out of control enough as it was. It just didn't appeal.

A couple of years ago I had every possible medical test going, and one of them was for my liver function. The doctor told me that I clearly wasn't drinking enough alcohol as I had a very healthy liver indeed. I am not quite sure how that can be, given the ease with which I was able to polish off a bottle of Marks and Spencer's Lambrusco bianco in my 20s, but there you have it.

Through reading about mental health I have discovered there is a very clear link between what we put into our bodies and our mental state. We need to nourish not just our bodies, but also our minds. It's all about the hippocampus, apparently – that's the part of the brain that is involved in memory, learning and also in mental disorders. Brains are, according to Associate Professor Felice Jackson, President of the International Society for Nutritional Psychiatry Research, highly sensitive to what we eat and the right balance is important for optimal mental functioning. There is a strong link between diet, anxiety and depression. Jackson explains that more than 90% of neurotransmitters like serotonin and dopamine are made in the gut, so maintaining a healthy gut can go some way to alleviating depression.

Very interesting, say I. What is more, a study in the European Journal of Clinical Nutrition found that middle-aged women who ate a mediterranean diet were less likely to have depressive symptoms after three years of follow up. So what we eat matters. It really matters. It makes total sense really. You just have to think about how you would feel after eating a fast food meal, as opposed to a nice salad niçoise or a just pink in the middle piece of salmon. There is no comparison. So I'll be trying to keep my crisp intake under control, and maximising my intake of fresh fruit and vegetables, which I have always enjoyed, whole grains, nuts, fish and the like. 'Eat what your grandmother would recognise,' is a good way of looking at it. That means getting rid of processed food, and eating more wholesomely.

A little bit of what you fancy, however, can be no bad thing. Dark chocolate is another weakness of mine, although I'm told it is actually quite good for you in small doses. I like the very high cocoa percentage stuff, so it's hard to eat too much of that, and I now find milk chocolate far too sweet.

Ian and I visited the Valrhona chocolate factory in the Rhone Valley earlier this year. That was a sensory experience way beyond anything I've ever had before. They do this amazing hot chocolate too, which we were fortunate enough to sample – think Juliette Binoche preparing her elixir in the movie *Chocolat* – great movie with Johnny Depp before he started getting all those dreadful tattoos. Loved him in *Pirates of the Caribbean*, but he doesn't need to look like a pirate in real life, with his tattoos, and his metal teeth and his multiple earrings. Johnny Johnny Johnny – you are getting old like the rest of us and you need to accept it. Look at George Clooney. Sexier than ever and not a tattoo in sight.

The whole culture of food and the social aspect of sharing food and drink is one of the great pleasures in life; it connects us to each other and to other cultures. I love the creative aspect of cooking and find it really therapeutic to spend time in the kitchen when I have the time and am not in a rush to get dinner on the table and feed two hungry boys.

The smell, the texture and the colour of food is all part of the experience. Who could fail to be enchanted by the red, green and white of a caprese salad, the vibrant yellow yolk of a farm-fresh boiled egg, the green of a just ripe enough avocado, the rich earthy hues of cumin and tumeric and cinnamon and chili, the rich reds and purples of berries, the yellows and oranges of mangoes, bananas, carrots and capsicums. Not only does food keep us alive, but it is a feast for all our senses and can make us very very happy.

> *Pull up a chair. Take a taste. Come join us.*
> *Life is so endlessly delicious.*
> ~ **Ruth Reichi**

Chapter 25
FINDING ACCEPTANCE

*Understanding is the first step to acceptance,
and only with acceptance can there be recovery.*
~ **JK Rowling, Harry Potter and the Goblet of Fire**

I have tried to build bridges with my family back in the UK. I am not sure if I have succeeded. Communication is sporadic. We see Facebook posts but don't have much meaningful contact. I love to write long emails, as I used to write letters, but we exchange these less and less. So I am trying to accept that we are not as close as I would like to be, trying to not get all worked up and anxious and filled with yearning for more meaningful, honest, open and transparent sibling connections. I can't spend time waiting for them to come and see me and wrap their hearts and minds around me in a warm fraternal or sisterly embrace. It's just not going to happen.

We all went through so much in the years after Dee died and both our parents were ill, but rather than bringing us together, their deaths seemed to push us further apart. That is, I feel further apart from my brother and sister; that may not be their perspective. I know they have been spending time together of late, so maybe the loss of Mum, Dad and Dee has brought them closer together. That's a good thing. I, though, am always aware of so much resentment bubbling beneath the surface of things said or unsaid, deeds done or not done, assumptions made, rightly or wrongly. But I'm hopeful that by the time I meet them again, the waters under the bridge will be less troubled and we will be able to share some happier times in the later stages of our lives. I hope that we won't drift further apart, now that my parents are no longer with us to bind us together in a very tenuous and often uncomfortable kind of way.

Mum was always telling me I had to be nice to my brother, and would get very cross with me if I said anything about him that wasn't one hundred percent positive. My mother never really understood sarcasm or appreciated my scintillating wit and would always get really defensive if she felt I didn't recognise my brother for the wonderful human being she considered him to be, what with his amazing career as a GP and all the charity work and fundraising he does for Nepal. My brother is indeed a good man, a family man through and through, immensely proud of his three children and growing brood of grandchildren. But human he is, and a bit of good-natured sparring is perfectly normal and a healthy part of any sibling relationship.

In the same way, Mum would never hear a bad word said about my eldest sister who died – all I wanted was to have truthful, honest and open conversations about what was going on but she perceived this to be unacceptable. I think Dee would have benefitted enormously from feeling she could open up and share all her demons with all of us, but sadly, that never happened.

My other sister, Lesley, is nine years older than me. We are not particularly close and travel to the beat of a different drum, although I do believe that she, like me, would like to rectify this. I have very fond memories of going to stay with her in London when I was still at school. I was crazy about football at the time, and even though it was not her thing at all she took me to watch a couple of First Division (EPL equivalent) games, much to my delight.

I was a very proud bridesmaid at her wedding but sadly, over the years we drifted apart and struggled to connect as I moved into adulthood. I used to think Lesley wasn't remotely interested in anything I had to say. I never felt that she really listened to me or looked on me as an equal. I have felt the same about my brother and often have the sense, whether real or imagined, that he looks down on me, that he judges me for simply being the way I am and that he doesn't value any of my ideas or opinions. But we probably have more in common than we all think. We both adore our spouses and children and have strong family values. Just because we live in different hemispheres and have very different tastes in most things doesn't mean that we can't find some common ground.

Lesley is retired now and recently moved up to Edinburgh. It's a city I've visited once with Ian while we were living in the North East of England and I'd like to go there again one day. My sister would be delighted to have me stay, of that I have no doubt. The last time we were together, after Mum had died, I was not in a good state. Well, neither of us were of course. I was expecting to catch a taxi from Heathrow to get to Mum's bedside as fast as I could, only to be met by Lesley and to find out that I was 12 hours too late. I was inconsolable, wracked with grief and guilt and regret. It was almost more than I was able to bear and, rather than finding solace amongst my family, being near them just served to remind me that I hadn't been there for Mum as she lay dying.

As the funeral and memorial service were being organised I felt like I was just there as a spare part, not as a participant in or contributor to all the arrangements that had to be made. It felt as if decisions were being made without my input, as if I was surplus to requirements, as if I had no right to have an opinion on anything as I was the 'little' sister who had moved to the other side of the world, who hadn't been there throughout Mum's illness or for her last days. In short, I felt like an impostor.

I have no doubt that both Tim and Lesley's recollection of events will be nothing like mine. But that was my reality at the time. It is amazing how people's perspective can be so divergent. At the time I felt hard done by; I'd had the shock of arriving at Heathrow only to be told Mum had died while I was in Dubai and I was too late. Of course we were all grieving, but my situation was slightly different. Tim and Lesley had been with Mum on her death bed, in her final hours. I had missed out. I was on my own, I didn't have Ian with me for comfort, I was exhausted from the flight, and arriving in the UK in the middle of winter at the start of the long WA summer is pretty depressing at the best of times. And for someone who is recovering from depression, who has just found out that she didn't arrive in time to see her mother alive again, it was a pretty grim situation all round. I just wanted to hide and sleep and not talk to anyone. I found no comfort in being around my family and felt very very lonely.

In our family we seem to be incapable of having a reasonable discussion in which we all give our points of view, are listened to with respect and feel our contribution is valued. At least that is how it is for me more often than not. Mum hated us to disagree on anything and always wanted us to convey some kind of a false air of family togetherness, which is absurd. We would be a lot closer now, I feel, if she'd just let us work things out in our own way, the way most siblings do. Thankfully, two of my closest friends, Julia and Lorna, came to see me one day in the aftermath of Mum's death, and a few hours spent with them restored my spirits to a large extent. The contrast with how I felt in their company, and how I felt in the company of my family, was striking. It made me very sad that things should be so, but I really didn't know what to do about it. At the time, I did try to break down some barriers, I really did, but I just seemed to keep hitting a brick wall and I simply didn't have the energy to persist.

I've recently had some email contact with my sister. I asked her if she could contribute her point of view so that I could include it in this book when I came to write about family. Actually, I didn't tell her I was writing a book, I told her I was working on a project. This book may never be published and she may therefore never read it, but she'll probably hate me again if she does ever read it. Which would be a real shame. I love my sister, she is the only one I have now, and I'd love to be closer to her. I'd love to be able to pick up the phone and just talk about this, that or the other. I'd love to share recipes with her and our views on having adult children and just generally have a sister who could be a confidante and who would treat me as a friend and an equal and really listen to what I have to say, and value my opinions. It astonishes me how our position in the family – Lesley as the big sister, Tim as the big (and only) brother, and me as the little sister – still has such a hold and influence on family dynamics even though we are now in our 50s and 60s.

With none of the family baggage that I carry around with me, Daniel stayed with my sister in Edinburgh recently when he was travelling around Europe and that made me very happy. He had a lovely time, she really looked after him and was extremely helpful, including going to pick him up when he missed the last bus home, and forwarding the credit card he left at their house to his next port of call, all when she was in a rush to get to the airport to go somewhere herself. I don't know if I would have been so accommodating. I know that it would have made her happy to have her nephew staying and to be able to do what she could for him.

When I asked Tim and Lesley to contribute their views on our strange family dynamics, I didn't hear back from Tim; his wife later emailed to say that it brought back too many bad memories, which I completely respect. I hope that he, in turn, will respect my need to write about family matters. Lesley took the time to respond and I was very moved by what she wrote. One of the things I asked was how it had affected her when I was going through my depression but she said that she really didn't know about it. My parents kind of knew, I'd tried telling them, but it was difficult as they themselves were very unwell at that time, and I was feeling somewhat ashamed of my mental state when they were battling physical illness. My mother's reply when I told her that I was depressed was "Oh, take a pill," and that was about it.

I never talked to Dad about it but if I had I suspect he would have said "this too shall pass," which would have been absolutely right, but I would have preferred to have a full conversation with him about it nonetheless. My parents never told either my sister or brother. My sister told me that she found it a very strange thing that they chose not to tell the others about my depression, but it pretty much sums up my family. Communication is not our strong point, but in not telling them, it was as if depression was something shameful that needed to be kept hidden. And it had the knock-on effect of making me feel that my family were not there for me, and weren't supportive when I needed them most.

I tried to tell my brother at one point but he really didn't want to hear about it. Which shocked and upset me hugely. There have been times when he has really helped me out, but on this occasion I felt like he was shutting me down. I realise now that he was probably dealing with his own issues and he just wasn't able, willing or ready to be there for his sister in the way that I wanted and needed him to be, but it still upsets me when I think about it.

Neither my brother or sister have any idea what it was like when my world fell apart. My brother had a heart attack about a year before. He recovered well but it was clearly a huge shock for him and the family for this to happen while he was still in his fifties. It reinforced, though, how much more seriously people seem to take physical illness. I remember being told that 'he'd had a heart attack for God's sake' when I was trying to explain what I had experienced. It was clear that my condition was of minor importance, and I failed miserably to elicit much sympathy for my fragile mental state. Thankfully I had other people who supported me and understood, including my parents-in-law who were simply wonderful, but there is something very sad about not feeling able to turn to your blood relatives in times of need, secure in the knowledge that you will be listened to without blame or judgement.

Lesley had lots of issues over the years about our older sister Dee. They were only three years apart in age, and had been close as children, and when Dee became pregnant Lesley was devastated. It had a huge impact on her own relationships with men until she met her husband to whom she has been happily married for over thirty years. Whenever I see them together, I am struck by their devotion to each other.

Lesley was very angry about Dee's alcoholism, the secrecy surrounding it, and the effect it had on Mum and Dad, but also feels guilty about the fact that her own life has turned out so well and now feels responsible for Dee's children and grandchildren. She has been through a lot of anger and guilt and painful emotions. I am so grateful Lesley has such a supportive husband who has allowed her to express all the angst caused by our family dynamics.

If Dee were alive today she would be a grandmother of four. I find it very sad that she didn't live to see her grandchildren grow up. They are quite prolific breeders, my nephews and nieces. I am now a great aunt nine times over. I haven't met the two who live in the US, but I am sure they are delightful children, as are the seven who live in England. My niece, Corinne, had problems conceiving and after several attempts at IVF gave birth to her beautiful daughter Emily who I only know through Facebook. My nephew Robbie, who stayed with us in 2010 and of whom my boys are very fond, is due to become a father early next year. His brother Philip, another lovely man, is a father of three. I hope we will get to meet them all again soon.

I don't know Lesley's children so well, and I know she is not happy about this and feels that her side of the family has been neglected. I feel that it is more a matter of geography and opportunity than neglect. We live so far apart and lead very different lives. My brother's three children have all been out to visit us in Perth so we naturally have closer bonds with them. My eldest sister's eldest boy lives on the edge of the Peak District with his wife and two boys. I've seen them occasionally. I used to feel very close to him but after we emigrated to Australia we lost touch to a large extent. I flew back for his wedding and have seen him occasionally over the years. It would be nice to see more of him.

The good thing is that my brother, my sister and I all have great relationships with our own children and I think that, given the way we were brought up and the example we were set, we should all be immensely proud of this. To the best of my knowledge we are all happily married, although marriage does of course have its ups and downs. My brother and his wife are doting grandparents and are making the most of this stage in their lives when they have more time to spend with their increasing brood. My two boys and their cousins get along really well and have very normal relationships. They don't know my sister's children well, but they have spent quite a lot of time with my brother's three children over the last ten years.

Daniel, in particular, has a good relationship with my brother and his wife. Last year he flew to Kathmandu to join Tim on one of his many visits to Nepal and absolutely loved it. When he was ten he came to France with me on a school trip and my sister-in-law met us at Charles de Gaulle airport and took Daniel back to England with her to spend a month with them in Bristol. He had the most wonderful time. It was an iconic moment in his young life, and the beginning of his love affair with travel and spirit of adventure I think.

He spent time getting to know his cousins and everyone looked after him so well. This was shortly after my brother had been out to stay with us in Perth and we had spent a lovely few weeks together over the Christmas period. Subsequently we all travelled back to the UK for a couple of Christmases, so we have had good times. It has not all been doom and gloom. But after my sister died, tensions resurfaced and we all had a few turbulent years in one way or another. I hope, though, that our baggage will now be lighter, that the pain and misunderstanding of the past will lessen with time, and we will find some kind of resolution and acceptance.

And what of my parents? I've said enough about what they didn't do, what they didn't teach me. I've written enough about their failings as parents. Maybe I have been far too critical. Who I am to judge? None of us are perfect parents. There is no point focusing on how I would have liked our relationship to be. I have to accept how it was. In my previously mentioned eulogy for Dad I focused on the positive and wrote about all the things I have to thank him for. Mum loved it, and I was glad that I was able to offer some comfort from the other side of the world. In a way I now understand why my brother and sister told me it was as if I was writing about a different man, because we all had a very different relationship with Dad. But what I wrote came straight from my heart and I meant every word.

I wrote about how accepting Dad had been about my move to Australia. Before I left he had told me, quietly but very firmly as was his way, not to think about coming back to England to visit, certainly not while I had a young family, to enjoy and build my new life down under and not look back. I remember that as the taxi pulled away from their house to take us to the airport I did look back and wondered if I would ever see him again.

Little did I know he would spend the next seven English winters under the Australian sun with us in Perth. I could have never foreseen that he and Mum would have so warmly embraced all that Australia has to offer, relishing the wide open spaces and bright landscapes. After all, there was not a stately home in sight, no castles, no mountains to climb.

In true Dad style, he was soon part of the local historical society and had joined the University of the Third Age at UWA where he would give lectures and poetry lessons to lesser-educated colonials. Their days in Perth were always full as Dad and Mum took themselves off to places I have yet to visit, including a Benedictine Monastery and a tiny chapel in the Swan Valley which they loved. They also loved the grandeur, peace and serene beauty of Kings Park, the Victorian charm of Fremantle and each day would regale me with more historical facts about 'my' city.

And then of course there was the beach. Dad would make his daily pilgrimage to one of the many Perth beaches, Cottesloe being a favourite, where he would, contrary to best medical practice and my advice, delight in soaking up the rays for hours on end. He was quite probably the only person left on the beach at midday. Perhaps the saying should be amended to 'Mad dogs and Irishmen …' Oh how Dad loved the sun, the sea the sand and the beach.

I am eternally grateful for what I call the Perth years, as Dad and Mum got to know my two boys who now remember them with such fondness. Daniel, my dreamer, my wise and thoughtful soul, remembers his grandad as being a gentle, soft, warm and kind man who stroked his head at bedtimes and never tired of reading him stories. Ben was only a baby when my parents first visited, so his memories are less concrete, but he remembers clearly how much Dad loved his garden when we visited them in England. Dad was by then already quite frail but each day was determined to tend and care for his plants and Ben loved going outside with him to help with watering and weeding and learn about the different flowers and produce. Ian came to develop a huge respect for Dad's intellect, his calm quiet demeanour. Because of Dad, Ian now keeps a copy of the meditations of Marcus Aurelius at his bedside.

The mention of gardening took me back to my childhood when Dad had an allotment – the plot as we called it – where I loved to spend time with him each summer, ostensibly to help but in reality to eat as many of the juicy green peas and plump red strawberries as I could. Dad worked tirelessly, lovingly tending his fruit and vegetables to provide his family with fresh healthy food (to counteract all the fry ups) and took great pride in it.

As children, we had amazing holidays each summer in the South of Ireland. With not a lot of money available Mum and Dad were still able to provide us with the best holidays ever, and these remain firmly engraved in my memory and my soul. Simple holidays and simple pleasures provided such wonderful, happy childhood memories which instilled in me a lifelong love of the ocean and the beauty of the natural world. The sea is part of me. One of my earliest memories is of Dad holding my hand and us jumping over the waves together, as well as splashing him vigorously in between jumps, with many screams and yelps as I did it. On the day he died I went down to the beach on my own and jumped over the waves.

In my eulogy I thanked Dad for making me who I am today. Despite trying to dissuade me from becoming a teacher, as he felt that teaching was not 'what it used to be,' this is what I became, and a finer profession there could not be. He was wrong. Teaching may have changed in many ways, but the essence of teaching remains the same; a profound love of learning, the pursuit of excellence, the joy of knowledge for its own sake and the belief that young people need to be nurtured, nourished, taught and guided, as they are the future. These things are unchanging and I am proud to continue his legacy as an educator although I could never match him as a scholar. I thank my dad for telling me there is no such word as 'can't,' for teaching me to hit the hockey ball as hard as I could, for the education he gave me, for nursing me when I was sick, for taking me to France, for doing the very best he could. I also have Dad to thank for what some might call my stubborn streak.

We all had very different relationships with our parents, so in a sense we were mourning different people. At Mum's memorial service, we all spoke and we all said very different things about Mum. Again, I focused on the happy, mostly childhood, memories I have of Mum and the things that we share, such as a love of books, learning and the beauty of nature. I spoke to a friend about this recently. She found, in the aftermath of her father's death, that she and her four siblings weren't brought together by their grief, because they didn't share the same relationship, and they weren't necessarily a comfort to each other. And so it was in my family.

I didn't get to say a proper goodbye to Mum, Dad and Dee. I wasn't with them when they died. When I last saw Mum, I read her a poem I'd written about her life. I read it to her just before I got on a plane to fly back to Australia. It was the last time I saw her. I really thought that I would see her again; there was supposed to be a sequel to the poem but she died before I wrote the next part. But we shared some special times that last summer in England and I'm trying to be content with that, to consider it to be enough. For it can never change. That was the way it happened and that is the way it will always be. I never saw her alive again, but when I left her I think she was happy with the time we spent together.

As I write this I find myself again wanting to remember the good times with them, the carefree days of childhood, the long summer holidays in France and Ireland, the seven summers they spent with us in Perth, sunburn and all. Life after loss is a strange thing. I always thought grief was a series of stages you had to go through, a progression of emotions, but the reality is that I have found myself moving in and out of my grief – going back and forward. I have learnt to adapt to it and to accommodate it into my life, but sometimes I am hit by a wave of sadness so powerful that I can barely stand.

I think of the dreadful waste of my sister's life, of the pain and suffering she tried to mask with alcohol until her body could take it no more, and it makes me weep. And my parents, they were good people. They lived their lives by a strict code but they were essentially good people. They were my parents, they gave me life, and I love them. I hope they are resting in peace together.

Any problem, big or small, within a family, always seems to start with bad communication. Someone isn't listening.
~ **Emma Thompson**

Chapter 26
BEYOND BUSY

*Never get so busy making a living
that you forget to make a life.*

~ **Dolly Parton**

I recently received an email from a former colleague who signed off with 'hope you are happy and busy.' Happy? I'm getting there. Contentment is good, I'll settle for contentment. Hugh Mackay argues that society's obsession with being happy, that everyone has the right to be happy, is in fact the root of many of our problems. I'm with Hugh on this one. In a recent article, Magda Szubanski said, 'I think this insistence on always being happy, I find it really boring. It can lack soul. Not that you court unhappiness but life is complex and life can be tough.' The pursuit of happiness – that's a whole other book that someone else has already written far better than I ever could. But busy? I'm so over busy. Busy is way overrated. I wondered what she meant. Was she saying that being busy makes us happy? Or makes us better people? Or, makes us more important and successful perhaps?

I think there is a lot of ego involved with saying we are really busy all the time. It is as if it gives you some sort of superior social status. We mistakenly think we need to be in a state of constant busyness in order to live a full life. I find the opposite to be true. In my experience, busyness often leads to exhaustion, if not burn-out.

How many conversations have you had in which you ask people how they are and the first thing they say is 'busy?' People often ask me what I'm doing now, as opposed to when I was working full-time, and rather than reply that I'm actually very much enjoying being less busy, I somehow find myself reeling off a list of work commitments, events and activities as if to justify my very existence. They then seem satisfied that I'm not sitting around idly painting my toenails or plucking out my navel fluff and cheerfully reply "Oh really busy then. Me too. I've got so much to do, I can't believe how busy I am these days," as if it is some sort of competitive sport.

As an introvert, I'm really good at being on my own and I need time on my own if I am to work effectively. Being busy all the time prevents us from achieving the level of mindfulness that is so beneficial for our mental health. If we have no time to reflect and simply be, for at least some of the time each day, how can we be fully present in our lives? There is a leisure researcher called Ben Hunnicutt – what a great job, I want that job – who outlines the importance of being able to refresh the soul by doing something purely for that reason, to restore balance, harmony and well-being.

The Greeks considered leisure as important as learning, time to reflect and think and pursue recreational activities. It didn't quite prevent the economic breakdown of their country did it, but hey, the idea was good. Bertrand Russell wrote that having the time to reflect leads to greater creativity in the arts, philosophy and sciences. While sharing some of his thoughts about life and the universe at the talk I attended recently, Tim

Winton compared writing with surfing. As a surfer, he spends a lot of time bobbing up and down in the water, waiting for the next perfect wave to appear on the horizon, and as a writer a lot of time is spent in reflection and thought, not actually writing, waiting for inspiration to strike, a new idea to unfurl, the latest character to take shape or that perfect sentence to form in our head. We all need that in our lives, the time and space to think and reflect. We all need more time to bob up and down in the waves.

 I attended a talk about the Danish concept of *Hygge* at the Perth Writers' Festival recently. Those Danes have it all worked out. They work a thirty-seven hour week and have six weeks of paid holiday per year. Leisure activities and time for friends and family are highly valued. Men and women share their lives and work an equal amount. Danish children are amongst the happiest in the world, they have a brilliant educational system and on top of that the economy is strong, unemployment is low, and the standard of living very high. They believe that money buys neither happiness nor time, and that work should not mean sacrificing your free time.

 Employers believe that holidays and leisure time make you not only a happier person but a better worker. Hallelujah. Praise the Lord. I want to live in Denmark. Actually, I don't really, I couldn't deal with those dark winter months and I'm not a fan of raw fish. But why can't we be more like the Danish right here in sunny WA? Why can't employers see that busy is not better. Why can't they see that busyness is not a good thing. And the merit certificate for the busiest employee this week goes to Neil from HR. No, no, no. No. And again no. This is not the way to live. Busyness is damaging and we fail to repair that damage at our peril.

Living on high alert all the time is most definitely not what the doctor ordered. We need time out. We can't keep a hundred balls in the air all the time. Leaving work on time, or god forbid, early, should not be frowned upon. It should be encouraged so that workers stay mentally healthy, productive, motivated and boost the morale of everyone – themselves included. Working long hours should be discouraged, if not stigmatised. It doesn't make us better people. Work smarter, not longer. Please listen employers, please listen to me.

Phew, I got myself quite worked up there. And I'm not even standing on a soap box. The point is, being busy is not necessarily a good thing for all people. Some people love it, some thrive on it, some love to brag about it, but I'm pretty sure the majority of people would much prefer to be a lot less busy. At worst, being too busy all the time leads to stress, and stress is not good for our brains, to such an extent that it actually causes them to shrink. I need as much of my brain as possible thank you very much.

The good news is that at the other end of the spectrum brain plasticity means that our brains can grow and become more effective, even as we age. A little bit of stress is a normal part of life but too much stress can lead to anxiety and depression, particular amongst women as we are more prone to these conditions. I learnt all this the hard way. And just as Taylor Swift is never ever ever getting back together with Harry Styles or whoever it was she was singing about (I'm pretty sure it was Harry) I'm never ever ever going there again.

> *Those who are wise won't be busy,*
> *and those who are too busy can't be wise.*
> ~ **Lin Yutang, *The Importance of Living***

Chapter 27
BEYOND TECHNOLOGY

We can't jump off bridges anymore because our iPhones will get ruined. We can't take skinny dips in the ocean because there's no service on the beach and adventures aren't real unless they're on Instagram. Technology has doomed the spontaneity of adventure and we're helping destroy it every time we Google, check-in, and hashtag.

~ **Jeremy Glass**

I often wonder why, when we are all supposedly more connected than ever before, the world seems to be more fractured, conflicted and divided than it's ever been. Technology is great. It's really, really great for finding stuff out and staying in touch with people and booking tickets and flights and holidays and the like. I love that I can listen to any radio station I want, stream any song that takes my fancy and have virtually the last half century of films at my fingertips. I love that I can listen to French all day long if I want to. I love the quality of photographs that I can take on my iphone and all the other amazing things it can do, even though I only use a miniscule amount of those.

But I'm not a slave to my phone. I actually prefer to keep a proper diary and I don't take my phone with me everywhere

I go. I don't want to be constantly answering texts when I'm on holiday or out walking. What is this modern compulsion for us to be in touch twenty-four hours a day, seven days a week when we are travelling? We survived for thousands of years without smart phones, and the world didn't stop spinning.

When I was travelling around Europe as a student we used to have to go to a post office, buy a token and then stand in a queue if we wanted to make a phone call. We used the poste restante service to receive letters, and were thrilled if there was a long awaited crisp blue airmail envelope waiting for us when we arrived in a new place. It all seems so quaint now, but rather romantic and sweetly nostalgic. And we not only survived, we thrived in the world prior to non-stop connection.

When I started taking school groups to France, mobile phones were not quite so ubiquitous, but each year they became more common, and each year I would have to answer questions from parents about how they could contact their little darlings while they were in France. I have very strong views on this. If parents are going to send their children on an educational visit to France, the last thing they should want their children to do is phone home. Nor should the parents be contacting them.

Hey, parents, leave your kids alone. Let them explore and discover the world. Let them immerse themselves in the language and culture. By all means, a text here and there to say that all is well, but that's enough. I once had a parent call me in Paris and question me as to why his daughter hadn't yet been to the top of the Eiffel Tower. We had only been there a couple of days. I had a school principal call me, because she had been contacted by a parent, whose child had phoned home from France because she was allergic to the cat belonging to her host family and needed to go to the doctor.

What could her parent possibly do about it and why call the principal who was probably somewhere lovely enjoying a well-earned break?

Oh yes, mobile phones have a lot to answer for. Complicating my life for a start, when I'm trying to run a French tour. We use them all the time because we can, not because we need to. What has happened to us? Look at us travelling on public transport, our minds buried in our phones, our eyes staring down at the endless overloaded stream of messages and information. Look up people, I want to shout, look out of the window of the bus, pull your head and eyes out of the latest *Bachelor* or *Bachelorette* gossip. (Yes, I know. I'm a complete and utter hypocrite.)

It's springtime in Western Australia as I write this, and on every patch of green there is a riot of glorious colour. Raise your eyes, open your mind. Who cares who Richie chose? Wars are breaking out all over the world, people are displaced, starving, and there is Richie with his smug face and perfect abs, and everyone is talking and writing about him, he's the man of the moment, the talk of the town. And as for that love-rat Blake – well don't get me started. Sounding a little judgemental there are we, Sue? Not that I ever watch reality TV, not me, no never watch reality TV.

Actually I do have a soft spot for *Survivor* – not the Australian version, although this last one was pretty compelling towards the end, but those early American ones, the ones with characters like Boston Rob and Amber – remember them? – I was obsessed with them. They were so beautiful to look at. How do people stay looking so damn good on *Survivor*? I'd be an absolutely frightful sight after forty days in the wilderness. They must have people on hand to carefully tousle their hair to create that perfect *Survivor* dishevelled look. Maybe I should apply to go on the next series – a few weeks eating nothing but witchetty grubs might help shift some of this stuff that's happening around my middle. On second thoughts, perhaps not; I'd be that really annoying middle-aged person that always gets voted out first and no-one wants to watch because she's not wearing an incy wincy, teeny weeny bikini.

Wow, where did that come from? Stay on track Sue. Back to phones. It is tempting to check messages throughout the day but I find it intrusive and counterproductive in the long run. Better to have a daily routine, a bit like going to the mailbox to collect the mail each day and devoting half an hour or so to opening letters and attending to bills. That's what I'm aiming for. I don't always achieve it but on the days that I do, I feel so much more in control of my life somehow, and less a slave to the beeping and pinging as messages come and go.

I also like to switch off the sound a lot of the time. The same with my computer or laptop. When I am writing, I'm training myself to switch off the Internet so that I am not constantly interrupted. I don't need to know that Myer are having yet another 50% off sale or what I can do with my Flybuys (does anyone ever use those? I haven't really got to grips with it. Probably missed out on lots and lots of stuff. More a Myer One girl myself). I don't want to know what amazing deals Booking.com have for me or how to decorate my house in true Parisian style – well actually maybe I would quite like to know about that but I can find out about it when I'm good and ready thank you very much.

I was wary about the tidal wave of technology that hit schools. I want to be able to decide how best to teach my subject and felt like I was one of the few people that didn't want to mindlessly follow the Pied Piper over the cliff into a brave new cyberworld that was nothing but a mirage. A few mixed metaphors there I'm sure but hey, that's a forte of mine as you already know. The only 'device' they really need is their brains. Staring at a screen for the duration of a lesson does not, in my very humble opinion, do anything to increase brain power. In fact, it has the opposite effect. It's hard enough for adults to resist the temptation to check emails and texts and messages and Facebook and Twitter throughout a normal working day. How much harder for adolescents with their still-developing brains? I know things are moving forward at a rate of knots but I have found that even with the most meticulously planned lesson filled with carefully scaffolded activities offering a range of differentiated outcomes, something will go wrong with the technology. Someone's stylus won't work, someone will need to charge their 'device' – some schools even give these a special acronym like PPD – personal pedagogical devices – what the fuck is that all about? That's what your brain is for. And call it what it is, a fucking laptop or an iPad not a fucking PPD puulease – give me strength.

"Excuse me, Madame, my PPD has stopped working so can I please go to ICT and can you please sign my PDR so that I can take it to the SLC and get permission to access one of the TEs in ICT?"

"Sure Cooper," I say with a sigh, "I'll see you tomorrow," I say, knowing that there is no way he will make it back to the classroom by the end of the lesson.

Languages are all about human interaction and personal connection. I have seen no evidence to suggest that having a computer on each school desk improves performance. Better to use precious classroom time in other ways and save the bulk of computer work for homework when students can do it in their own time when it's their problem if things don't work.

Students need human engagement, they need to feed off the ideas of their peers, they need occasionally to listen to me and reap the benefits of my encyclopedic knowledge, peppered of course with the odd hilarious joke or well-observed anecdote. I've wasted so much class time trying to sort out everyone's technology issues. We are not technology experts. We are experts in our subjects but now, on top of everything else we are expected not only to have Bill Gates' passion for all things IT but also to be really good at it. And that's just not possible. We simply do not have the time.

One day recently, in one of the schools where I work as a relief teacher, I had a couple of weeks in which the laptops were all getting a work out during every lesson in line with school policy – apart from those whose stylus was broken or whose battery was flat, or whose OneNote wouldn't load – I'm a bloody language teacher not a techy, nerdy type of person for God's sake. I don't expect computer geeks to be experts on 17th century French tragedy or the theory of the absurd, do I? So why am I expected to be able to seamlessly negotiate the ever-changing world of updates and applications and cyberspace?

Anyway, one day the students said to me at the start of their lesson "Can we please not use our laptops today? Could you please just teach us?" I rest my case.

So much wasted time. There is a lot to be said for "come in, take your seats and turn to page 38." It's old fashioned but it gets the students working right from the start of the lesson. No need to wrestle with computer bags and cords and finding a power socket. The worst kind of class I've had to cover as a relief teacher is last period of the day, RAVE, with the instruction 'students are to continue their research project on Siddartha.' I'm pretty good at it now. I know, inevitably, that half the class will need to charge their computers, which will involve going to lockers and lots of time-wasting so I come prepared with my own spiel about Buddhism, about which I know very little really but I've been to India so I can entertain them with my travel tales and what little I know about the Noble Eightfold Path to Enlightenment. It usually goes down pretty well. They know I am a French teacher but one student recently asked me if I was now a teacher of religion, so I'll take that as a win. Keep it simple stupid, that's my motto.

I'm not against technology by any means. It's not just the future, it's the here and now. I know all students need to be proficient in digital technology to equip them for their working lives in the digital world beyond school. The problem is that I don't think we have been going about this the right way. Putting a digital device on every child's desk and expecting each teacher to somehow seamlessly merge the pedagogical, technological and content knowledge required for effective teaching in our modern classroom is simply not working. We need more training, we need more time, and there is no time, because we are so busy trying to plough through the syllabus in our own subject areas.

Little old me is woefully underprepared and lacking the knowledge to teach Johnny much about completing challenging digital tasks. And yet, embedded in our Australian Curriculum is the assumption that all teachers across all subject areas will contribute to the development of our students' digital knowledge and skill. This sounds great, as do many things in theory, but it is simply not practical. And sure enough, national data released last year, based on a survey of some ten thousand students, indicates that despite the enormous amount of money invested in digitalising every classroom, around half of all secondary school students fail to meet the minimum requirements in digital literacy. This is crazy.

I believe that experts in the field need to be teaching ICT or digital literacy or whatever the hell it is called, as a separate compulsory subject, just like English and Maths. It shouldn't just be tacked on as something the average teacher is expected to master and disseminate. There, that's my little rant about technology in schools. Let's move on.

How we use technology in schools, and how we use it in our everyday lives, are completely different things. Despite some of my misgivings, I'm pretty attached to my iphone, and I have my very own contact at the Apple shop in Perth. One of my ex-students works there and I think of her as my personal Apple shopper. She's called Sammy and she is the most lovely girl. I'm enormously fond of her. We even have coffee together now and again. She came with me on one of my French trips so our connection goes way beyond the classroom, and on top of that I taught her from Year 3 to Year 12 so we got to know each other pretty well.

I am the main source of all her linguistic knowledge, which is a bit of a scary thought. She would be the first to admit that she wasn't a top student but she is one of the most positive students I have ever taught, always smiling, never complaining. When the latest iphones came out I was in the market for a new one. Sammy let me know so that I could go in to the shop when all the initial hullabaloo had died down and it was less busy. There were a couple more of my former students working there on that occasion and we had a good laugh about how the tables had turned and they were now the experts teaching me how to use my new phone and doing all the setting up while I listened attentively and tried to remember everything. Even funnier that one of the topics on the French syllabus when I taught them in Year 12 was technology and they had to be able to talk about how they used their mobile phones in French.

Anyway, with my new iphone I took the most magnificent photos in France earlier this year and finally decided to join the Facebook community so that I could share my photographic masterpieces with the world – well with about sixty-five friends to be precise. Apparently though, Facebook is sooo 2014 and it's all about tweeting, instagraming, tumbling and snapchatting now. Facebook has become the cyber playground of the middle-aged.

While technology can waste so much time in the classroom, and needs rethinking in my very humble opinion, the Internet has opened up a wonderful world of knowledge. In my subject, technology connects us to other languages in ways that I could never have imagined when I was trying to master the perfect tense or the present subjunctive. I remember staying up late to watch French films on BBC 2, films that improved not only my language skills but educated me far more than my parents ever did about the ways of the world. Today, I have every French film I could ever want to watch at my fingertips, every radio and TV station. It's quite astounding when you think about how much progress has been made in such a short time.

Children today spend most of their free time staring at a screen. In fact, come to think of it, the classroom could be the only place where they are actually forced to listen to someone speaking and have two-way conversations that don't involve a keyboard of some sort and good old fashioned face to face human interaction, and sit in groups and work things out together by actually talking.

Babies these days have an iphone shoved into their wrinkly little hands as soon as they emerge from the womb for God's sake. They are playing computer games long before they are toilet trained. A survey of Australian children recently stated that children spend an average of 30 percent of their waking hours at weekends in front of a screen – 3 hours a day on average during the week and 4 hours on average at the weekend, and those are conservative estimates. If you add in time at school that doesn't leave a lot of time for healthy outdoor play and other activities.

Witnessing a toddler tantrum in the supermarket one day, not because the toddler was being denied a treat but because she wanted to use her mother's iphone, was an extremely dispiriting sight, which did nothing to make me feel optimistic about the future of the human race. It makes me laugh, or perhaps it should make me cry, when I read about some recent survey claiming there is a link between screen time and physical well-being. Well knock me down with a feather. Professors and researchers are being paid thousands of dollars for coming up with a conclusion that any person with half a brain should have made long ago. It's so damn obvious.

Regardless of any formal research, instinctively I know that reliance on computers in the classroom as the main method of disseminating content is not a healthy thing. This does not mean students shouldn't learn how to use computers at school, just, as I've said before, that how we do this is not working at the moment, and they need to be taught how to do it by experts in the field.

A 2013 Canadian study reports that the use of pen and paper outperforms technology in promoting understanding and memory recall. Writing things down, processing what is said, rewriting what you have heard in your own words, all these things require careful attention. And technology interferes with our attention, it diminishes, or even impedes completely our capacity to reason, problem solve and learn language. It alters perception and stunts creativity. It is now also acknowledged that screen time has a detrimental effect on children's ability to master their emotions and delay gratification, as well as to read faces and body language.

OK Sue, enough, you can get off your hobby horse now, I hear you say. Isn't this supposed to be a book about your journey through anxiety and depression, not about how much Steve Jobs and Bill Gates have to answer for. The point is that I'm not against technology per se. I just don't want to be dictated to, and in my own life I'm very aware of the detrimental effect it can have on me, so we need to protect our children from that and teach them what we know, because we do know a bit of stuff. That's what I object to – this assumption that every classroom has to be super digital and that if it isn't we are behind the times. That's simply not the case.

I use technology all the time. I'm sitting here at my laptop bashing out words at a rate of knots, far faster than I could when writing by hand – touch typing, one of the best things I ever learnt. Everyone should do it. But the Internet is off, I'm not checking my Facebook every ten minutes, there are no pop-ups and ads, and links all over the page. I'm fully focused on what I am doing.

And sure enough, a couple of years on there is an increasing body of research showing that I may have been right all along. I'm with John Vallance, the former Headmaster of Sydney Grammar School, who recently spoke up about the scandalous amount of money that has been wasted on technology in Australian schools. Researchers like Susan Greenfield believe technology is reshaping our brains. Internet addiction, excessive gaming, and mobile media multitasking have been linked to a decrease in grey matter intensity in the parts of the brain that regulate blood pressure, heart rate, empathy, will power and decision making and may even cause increased risk of depression, anxiety and other mental health conditions. That's huge. That's really huge. And mental health aside, it is so blatantly obvious that excessive interaction with screens has a negative impact on social skills. You don't need a scientific study to prove it. You just need to look around you.

Clearly, we need to proceed with caution, and reappraise the current state of affairs. One of the schools I teach in now gets the students to put their ipads in a box at the front of the class if they are not going be needed in the lesson – great – the temptation to sneakily go online is removed and we get on with the job. As teachers, we can offer some respite from the cyber world, we can insist on eye contact, face to face discussion and making hand-written notes. Yes, hand-writing, remember that? It has been proven to help retain information. Give a child a hand-out, or show them a PowerPoint and chances are they will retain very little. Ask them to make notes from the PowerPoint, handwritten notes and I don't know why, but there is something about the physical act of forming letters that become words which turn into sentences and paragraphs and essays, of actually forming those letters in ink, that helps to retain information.

I find it beyond alarming that there may very well be a link between screen use and psychological problems, including depression and even suicidal tendencies. Some worrying statistics are emerging suggesting a link between problematic Internet use, depressive disorders and even attempted suicide amongst 11–17 year olds. We need to be very, very careful in this relatively new and unchartered territory. Only time will reveal the potential long-term effects of our reliance on, and ubiquitous use of, technology.

Adult dependence is just as concerning. Maintaining our intellect is vital as we age. Rather than relying on Google, we need to keep storing information and memories in our brains as much as we can, and making our own intellectual connections to ensure our minds stay active and healthy into old age.

The whole social media stratosphere can be a great place to connect with others, and especially to keep in touch with friends and family we don't see often, but it needs to be used in moderation. When I first set up my Facebook account I could feel myself getting sucked in, checking more regularly, getting agitated if I hadn't posted yet another spectacular photograph taken in an area of outstanding natural beauty. We risk becoming observers of our own lives. Sometimes it's better to leave the phone at home or back in the hotel and really experience the day as it unfolds without distractions.

In being connected to the Internet all the time we often disconnect from all that is going on around us. My boys delight in mocking my use of social media, especially when I once posted a picture of a particularly delicious plate of food – something I used to be very scornful of in others.

"You are such a hypocrite, Mum," they will say.

"Ah, but the food was French so that's OK," say I, rather lamely.

Our obsession with capturing everything through a lens and posting it online often stops us from focusing on more important things. It takes so much time and energy to keep up a constant flow of tweets and snapchats and instagrams. I have no idea where people find the time to do it all. I'm all for sharing, but I'm not convinced the current social-media epidemic of oversharing is a good thing.

… Now where was that funny Youtube video about the singing cat? And why has no-one liked my latest Facebook post about how to make the perfect Victoria sponge?

> *We refuse to turn off our computers,*
> *turn off our phone, log off Facebook,*
> *and just sit in silence, because in those moments*
> *we might actually have to face up to who we really are.*
>
> ~ **Jefferson Bethke**

Chapter 28
BEYOND PERFECTION

If I waited for perfection ... I would never write a word.
~ **Margaret Atwood**

Although I have expressed my dislike for grandiose statements and the assumption that in order to be content we need to be jumping off the walls with excitement all of the time, and never experience any setbacks, I would be the first to admit that I don't always practise what I preach. As parents, we all, of course, want our children to be happy. Last Monday when I asked Ben how his day had been as he came through the door he told me that it had been "OK," to which I replied "Only OK?" He looked at me quizzically, said that I often asked this question and proceeded to elaborate quite cheerfully on his day. I felt bad about how I had reacted. He had clearly experienced a normal school day, things had gone well on the whole and he was fine.

That got me thinking. What's wrong with OK? Surely OK is fine, OK is good, OK is perfectly all right.

We have come to talk in superlatives. Everything has to be awesome, fabulous, beyond fantastic, to die for, and so on. The meaning of less spectacular adjectives such as 'nice,' 'fine' and 'satisfactory' has thereby been diminished. On hearing 'OK' the latent helicopter Mum in me thinks, why only OK? Did your teachers not praise you enough, did you not give the smartest answers, were you not the most popular boy in the school, surrounded by your peers during lunch time and recess hanging on your every word? To which he would reply if he could read my thoughts, "No, Mum, but it was fine, I had an OK day."

When I was at school, in the dim and very distant past, our termly reports were extremely concise. The comments I received ranged from 'very good' to 'good,' 'very satisfactory' and 'satisfactory.' To get a 'very good' was virtually unheard of. 'Good' meant that you were one of the top students. 'Satisfactory' that you were a solid performer. These days, at the merest whiff of the word 'satisfactory' a parent will pick up the phone to demand explanations. It is not uncommon for teachers to be asked to justify comments that reflect anything less than the wonderfulness of their child. However, on referring to the dictionary, satisfactory is defined as 'fulfilling expectations or needs' and synonyms include 'competent,' 'sufficiently good,' 'up to the mark,' 'up to standard.' Sounds perfectly fine to me.

I was recently working on a project and kept tweaking and redrafting more than was necessary. When talking about this to a friend who shares similar perfectionist tendencies, asking when I would know it was as good as it could be, she replied that she was learning to accept the concept of 'good enough.' The phrase defines itself – it's good, and it's enough. Time to finish and move on.

In our family we love to retell an incident in Daniel's childhood that illustrates such linguistic shades of meaning.

While staying with their grandparents my boys went with them to have lunch with some friends, one of whom is a Swiss-trained chef who has recently catered for no less than the great Antonio Carluccio at his boutique bed and breakfast. Steve, the chef, had made his signature crème anglaise to accompany dessert and when asked what he thought of the 'custard,' six-year-old Daniel thought for a moment and then replied, "It's good, but it's not fantastic." My in-laws drew in a sharp breath, there was a momentary pause, and then Steve's laughter broke the silence. He is known for his infectious laugh, so within seconds everyone had joined in and any potential discomfort had passed. 'Good but not fantastic' has become something of a catch phrase in our family. We have come to embrace 'good.'

I must remember this when my son tells me he is 'OK,' or 'good' – another of his common responses. After all, good was good enough for God when he was creating the world. For each of the first five days of creation God surveyed his work and 'saw that it was good.' Only on the sixth day, after lots of practice and achievement did God view all that he had made and deem it 'very good.' If it was good enough for the big man (person) in the sky, it should be good enough for us.

So as my son puts down his heavy school bag, picks up his enormous cricket bag, kisses me and heads off to the nets I know that he is indeed OK, he is fine, we talk and laugh every day and all is well in his world.

If you look for perfection, you'll never be content.
~ **Leo Tolstoy, *Anna Karenina***

Chapter 29
BEYOND NEGATIVITY

The primary cause of unhappiness is not the situation but your thoughts about it.
~ **Eckhart Tolle**

Changing old, negative thinking patterns does indeed take time, but we need to face this challenge if we are to stay mentally healthy. Just as clogged arteries can lead to a heart attack or stroke, or an excess of sugar can cause diabetes, the clogged thought pathways of the mind provide the perfect conditions for anxiety and depression to flourish.

I have always been a worrier, with perfectionist tendencies, fearful of the judgement of others and overly sensitive to criticism. I have learnt that people with my personality traits are more likely to experience depression and anxiety, and therefore changing the way I think became a crucial part of my recovery and ongoing well-being.

'If you do what you always did you'll get what you always got.' I often used to quote this saying to my students, when they kept behaving in the same way and then being surprised when they ended up with the same result. But in order to get to the point of being able to act and change what you do, you first need to be able to change the way you think. This may sound simple, but tackling years of limiting and destructive thought processes is easier said than done. Like any skill, it takes practice, and to practise you need time. To that quotation I would add 'If you think what you always thought, you'll do what you always did and you'll get what you always got.' The key is to change your thinking.

I have been to see a few psychologists over the years, but until I consulted Dr Sophie Henshaw (see chapter 11) I had never really clicked with any of them. I seemed to always find myself going round in circles, reliving old hurts, betrayals and losses and getting nowhere. At some point, as I was recovering from depression, I just felt that enough was enough. I was feeling sufficiently better to begin to care for myself. That is not to say there aren't some wonderful psychologists out there, doing amazing, often life-saving, work. I just didn't find one that I felt justified the hourly rate at that time. You can get a care plan which entitles you to some rebate, but even with that I didn't feel that the results I was achieving were commensurate with the outlay. I preferred to spend my money on things I love to do, in particular travel, which has been such an important part of my recovery. The first psychologist my GP referred me to after my diagnosis recommended that I buy and read a book called *Change your Thinking*. Great, I thought at the time, charge me $180 and then tell me to go out and spend another $35 on a book. I wasn't impressed.

The book, however, based around Cognitive Behavioural Therapy (CBT), was a good read, and the first of the many books I read on my road to recovery. I'm not going to go in to the whys and wherefores of CBT. There are plenty of books that do it far more effectively that I ever could. My take on CBT is that in the first instance, when you are in the grip of depression, you are really not in a position to embark on it with any kind of success. For me anyway, I didn't have sufficient concentration or focus until I began to emerge from the blackness. I had no inclination to read a book about changing my thinking.

But after a while I read the book. I already knew a lot of the principles from my work as a teacher, and I had done some counselling training along the way. I was lucky that to some extent I could use that knowledge to try to heal myself. It all sounds so easy on the surface but it is actually very difficult to change some fifty-four years of thinking patterns.

It's the same thing with the concept that happiness is a choice. I accept and understand that, and can rationalise all these excellent ideas, but it takes time to actually incorporate them fully into your life. It takes time and you have to do the work. As well as worrying about the future, focusing on past hurts, betrayals and injustices is not conducive to good mental health. CBT does not aim or claim to be able to remove all upsetting emotions or situations, but it can help us to respond in a less dramatic and self-destructive way.

Feelings of grief, or betrayal, or loss or hurt or disappointment or regret are emotions that arise as part of a normal life. But when they go unchecked, they can lead to intense anxiety, rather than a normal level of worry or concern, and depression, rather than an expected level of sadness. CBT does not mean that we cannot express our emotions, but it is a therapy that challenges our unhelpful thoughts and beliefs about any given situation so that we can respond more appropriately to difficult or stressful situations. This is at the core of CBT; people and events do not make us feel good or bad, it is the way in which we respond to them that determines how we feel.

CBT has been a useful tool for me and it is something you can learn to do yourself if you apply yourself fully to it, in the same way that you would study for an examination. You have to put the hours in and do the exercises and really, really want to change.

I did really want to change my tendency to worry and catastrophise. I wasted hours and hours worrying about resigning from my job in 2014. I was very upset about it, but on top of that I worried endlessly about the future. I was drained, exhausted, traumatised and on the verge of experiencing full-blown PTSD.

The day after I resigned, I had another job offer and then more opportunities arose, not just for work but also wonderful life-enhancing opportunities that would take me in different directions. I achieved a much better work-life balance, so all the worrying was for nothing. It was understandable to be traumatised and upset by the events that had taken place, but I made things harder for myself by rehashing the past and worrying about what would happen next. It was pointless. But it is in my nature, it is ingrained in me, and I still do it to some extent. I am still prone to overthinking and catastrophising, but I am much much better at getting things in perspective and much quicker at moving on. I can laugh about it, and the boys pick me up on my ridiculous 'what if' scenarios. So I would recommend CBT. A few sessions should be enough to set you on your way. And it all ties in beautifully with the Buddhist principal that we are what we think.

I don't completely agree with Shakespeare's assertion – or rather Hamlet's – that 'Nothing is either good or bad but thinking makes it so.' There is no getting away from the fact that some things simply are intrinsically bad, some situations are terribly difficult. But how we approach those things and those situations, how we think about them, can most definitely make them worse or better.

My experience with changing thinking patterns is that we need to go beyond our rational minds, into a place where we find the serenity to make that change a reality. And this is where practices such as yoga, meditation, mindfulness and breathing techniques can be so helpful in allowing us to transcend our rational minds and enter a realm where destructive and negative thoughts can be let go. Sometimes we can't avoid having such thoughts. The key is to be able to acknowledge them and then let them go before they take hold of our minds and cause the chaos and despair that can lead to depression and anxiety.

If you have good thoughts they'll shine on your face like sun beams and you will always look lovely.
~ **Roald Dahl**

Chapter 30
BEYOND BLAME

I wondered if that was how forgiveness budded; not with the fanfare of epiphany, but with pain gathering its things, packing up, and slipping away unannounced in the middle of the night.

~ **Khaled Hosseini**, *The Kite Runner*

When you go through a tough time you really find out who your friends are. I've heard many people who have experienced depression describe how some so-called friends just seemed to disappear into the woodwork. Why the woodwork? What's that expression all about? Anyway, I found that to be true. People respond very differently to physical and mental illness. Heart attacks, cancer, broken limbs, any range of physical conditions and people rally round, offering casseroles and bringing flowers and calling round regularly to visit and offer support. Not quite the same with the mental side of things. It makes a lot of people very uncomfortable.

It's hard not to feel hurt when people we thought we could rely on simply aren't there for us. I found it very hard, and for a while I was quite bitter and resentful about it. But holding on to outrage or anger, and indulging in convoluted revenge fantasies – as I did for a while – serves no purpose whatsoever and is detrimental to our own well-being. We need to let go of what was done and how we were then, and experience ourselves as we are now. We need to resist petulance. Life doesn't owe us anything. It is not the natural order of things that our lives should be lovely all of the time, and that people should behave as we want them to. If we are to grow and expand we need to forgive betrayals and hurts so that we can be free. We need to forgive life for not always working out the way we would wish. We need to forgive ourselves for our failings.

As soon as I let go of what I perceived to be the wrongdoings of others I woke up to a deeper sense of purpose in my life. We need to cut the negative ties we have with those who hurt us. We can't assume to know what is going on in someone else's life, or understand why they act the way they do. For a while I lost all faith in humankind and in myself and I had never felt more alone. But eventually something shifted in me, and as I recovered I found within me the capacity to embrace life again, to trust again, and rediscovered the sheer joy of being alive. I returned my attention to those I love and began to focus more on all the positive things in my life. I stepped back from the need to get even and realised that here was an opportunity to gain knowledge and experience and find a renewed sense of purpose, and as I did this my sense of wonder returned a thousand fold.

I will never forget the day when I was feeling pretty desperate and a friend arrived on my doorstep like an angel sent from heaven. We were due to meet for coffee, but I was in a pretty dark place that day and had texted her to cancel. Half an hour later, there she was on my doorstep, gourmet lunch for two in hand. Such kindness.

I was going through a 'why is this happening to me' phase. It was around the time I'd found out I was on the verge of full blown PTSD. I kept saying to my friend over and over again, "I don't understand, I don't understand." Her response was to listen, let me cry and rant, and eventually she told me that I would never understand, that I had to stop trying to understand, and once I had processed that I found that I was able to let it go. We talked about how we all carry scars, but that they can heal. They stay there, like the scar I have on my wrist when I fell through a window while at university. And I wasn't even drunk. I just slipped on my bed and tried to break my fall by putting my arm against the wall and it went straight through the little window above my bed, a shard of glass piercing my wrist. It is hard to explain that scar on my wrist sometimes, but it was a complete accident.

So our scars remain, physical or mental, but they heal and become less obvious, and begin to fade with time to the point where we barely notice them. They are still there and they all contribute to who we are, but they don't have to hurt anymore. We can be reminded of how that scar got there, and sometimes there are echoes of the pain they caused at the time, but we can get to the stage where we think of that time with a sense of curiosity without the pain and upset that it used to cause. At least that is what I have found. In order to flourish we need to move beyond resentment and blame towards compassion, love, wonder and discovery.

> *... forgiveness neither begins nor ends with words ... far more important than words are the shifts in attitude those words accompany, the changed actions they allow, the compassion they elicit, and, ideally, the love they free to flow.*
> ~ **Stephanie Dowrick,**
> ***Forgiveness and Other Acts of Love***

Chapter 31
BEYOND FEAR

*Our doubts are traitors,
And make us lose the good we oft might win,
By fearing to attempt.*
~ **William Shakespeare**

Recently, I flew across the country to Melbourne for the weekend to attend a stand-up comedy masterclass. A strange thing to do, perhaps, when you are a shy, introverted, anxious kind of person recovering from major depression. Book yourself onto a comedy class where you'll have to stand up and do a three-minute comedy routine at the end of the day without notes. Actually, I didn't know that at the time of booking, otherwise I may well not have proceeded. It took me so far out of my comfort zone I was floating around in cyberspace with George Clooney and Sandra Bullock. (Yes, I know, I've used that line before, but I like it, and I've always loved GC and SB).

I love Melbourne, and every time I go there I feel instantly at home as I walk out of the airport and onto the Skybus. I've been visiting Melbourne ever since we arrived in Perth in 1999, often on my own to visit a very dear, wise, and wonderful friend. Every time I see her I feel uplifted and inspired. We met years ago in the UK when she did an exchange with one of the art teachers at the school where I was working. It was one of those fairly posh English public schools in a postcard-perfect village in the south east of the country. Somewhere south and east of Cambridge and north east of London.

Marita arrived in the village like a lightning bolt. She was exotic and different and wore bright clothes and bright lipstick and carried a wicker basket filled with interesting things to entertain the students who were lucky enough to be in her Junior School art classes. She fell in love with the place and the people and we all fell in love with her.

I first met Marita the day after she arrived. I was standing outside my 15th century Elizabethan cottage looking up and down the street. She lived across the road from my cottage in an apartment above the home of a lovely old lady called Enid. Marita is one of those people who takes an interest in absolutely everyone. Not because she is nosy or interfering but because she absolutely loves people. I had lived across the road from Enid for a year or so and hadn't bothered to knock on her door to introduce myself. Within a couple of days Marita and Enid were firm buddies. Enid will be long dead now, but they kept in touch for many years, long after Marita had returned to the land down under.

During a trip back to the UK a few years later Marita came to visit me. I'd swapped the school in the home counties for an equally lovely but slightly more rustic and rugged school in a market town in the North East of England. The school stood proudly on a hill with spectacular views across to the Yorkshire Dales. A Cathy and Heathcliff kind of scene.

Marita had found out that Enid was then living in the Lake District, about an hour's drive from me, so she borrowed my car one day, drove through snow, sleet and hail across the notorious A66 to get to Enid, who was overjoyed. They had a beautiful few hours drinking tea and eating scones and I have no doubt that seeing Marita again would have brightened her day. She would have been well into her 90s by then.

Anyway, on the day I met Marita she happened to glance out of her window, only to see little old me pacing around and looking anxiously up and down the street, and took it upon herself to come down and investigate. Turns out I was waiting for the delivery of some newly-acquired furniture. Some beautifully-crafted country pine furniture. Not the kind of mass produced slightly orange hued pine furniture you can buy so cheaply these days, but lovingly created items with tongue and groove joints, not just a couple of bits of MDF glued together.

The Elizabethan cottage I lived in at that time was tiny, so I could only fit in a couple of items, but when I moved into a bigger house in the aforementioned North East of England I ordered more from the same furniture maker. He and his wife drove it all up to us themselves, up the A1 to Scotch Corner and across the A66 and didn't charge us any extra for delivery. Talk about customer service! Harvey Norman could learn a thing or two. The furniture maker and his wife drove all day to get to us, just in time for the dinner party we were having that night, helping us set up the brand new eight-seater table and chairs.

I still have most of the pieces today, except for the six foot wardrobe, which I sold to a friend I met through the NCT when I was pregnant with Daniel. Not much call for such wardrobes in Australia. Everyone, well almost everyone, has built-in robes, some of which are so large and lavish they could house a family of refugees with room to spare. So no capacious pine wardrobes needed in Oz. But the rest of the furniture still looks great.

I went off it for a while and dreamt of more contemporary, streamlined minimalist pieces, but now I've grown to love it again. A bit like coming to love myself again. I wanted to be all contemporary and streamlined and chic and poised, but that's not me. I'm more like a solidly-built pine dresser. Not particularly chic or modern but very handsome in its own way, built to last, unfailingly reliable, loyal and dependable.

So Marita offered to wait for my furniture in my little Elizabethan cottage while I went off to do whatever very important and pressing thing it was I had to do that was making me so anxious about having to wait for the delivery. She made herself at home and we have been friends ever since. There have been times when we haven't seen each other for years. I got caught up in my new life in Perth, having children and making them tuna sandwiches – my son recently told me that I gave him tuna sandwiches pretty much every day for lunch throughout his primary school years. Tuna sandwiches and bananas, to which he now seemingly has a life-long aversion. Tuna he will still eat, but only when desperate. At least his omega 3 levels will be pretty high which might explain his sunny disposition. He had enough of the stuff between the ages of five and eleven to last a lifetime.

So while I was busy bringing up my family Marita and I rarely saw each other. But it is one of those friendships that is never in question, no matter how much time passes between visits. I have a few of those friendships, less than I could count on my fingers and toes, but they are so sustaining and life enhancing. Post-depression I have come to treasure those friendships more than ever before.

Marita is one in a million. She has no children and has never been married, but not once, not once, has she bemoaned the lack of progeny or spouse in her life. Marita looks around her and thinks, what can I do today, who can I visit, which museum should I explore, what lovely food can I make, how can I make this day the best day possible for me and everyone else around me? It's infectious. Not in an irritating Pollyannaish kind of way. She's also got a wicked sense of humour and doesn't mind a bit of salacious gossip now and then. There's a permanent twinkle in her eye and a big warm roaring fire in her heart. I love her to bits.

So apart from the comedy masterclass, Marita is in Melbourne, and I have other friends there too, and on top of that I'll take any chance going to get away from WA drivers for the weekend. WA, the state where merging, indicating and keeping left are about as likely as Jacquie Lambie and Pauline Hanson getting together over a nice Halal meal, or Donald Trump inviting all his Mexican friends over for tacos. I digress. The point is, I conquered my fear, went to Melbourne, did the eight-hour masterclass and the three-minute stand-up routine at the end. May or may not have 'died' but I don't really remember. On second thoughts, I did get a few laughs. But that's not the point. The point is that I did it. I stood up and spoke without notes for three minutes, something I have never ever done before and some of it may just have a been a tiny weeny bit funny. And nothing bad happened.

All through the day I'd kept looking around at everyone else. It was an eclectic group: quite a few teachers like me, an architect who had flown in from Brisbane – so I wasn't the only crazy person who came from interstate – a couple of climate change experts wanting some material to lighten up their presentations, a TV presenter, etc etc. A broad spectrum of people.

For some reason I always think everyone else knows more than me, will be better than me, will think badly of me, I am not worthy, I am not worthy, I am not worthy. But it wasn't like that at all. Everyone was nervous, we were all in the same boat. And that's the thing. We are all here trying to make sense of this earth and our place on it, and we are all equally worthy, and we all have a place. We just have to find the place where we feel most comfortable, the place where we can grow and flourish and be our absolute authentic selves.

At the end of that day I was elated. I'd learnt so much – not just from the fabulously amazing Rachel Berger who so generously and articulately shared her words of comedy wisdom, but also just by being there and doing it and breaking down a few of the barriers I create for myself, peeling away a few layers of my onion to reveal just a little glimpse of what might lie beneath. It had started when I read a book by the equally fabulous and amazing Catherine Deveny called *Use your Words*. Being an aspiring writer I've read a few writing self-help type books in my time, and none of them had clicked with me. In fact, I would often find myself reading the last page and proceeding to forget about writing for a while, so dispirited was I. More self-destruct than self-help. But when I finished Dev's book, I sat down at my computer and proceeded to write over ten thousand words in a few days. This woman might just know a thing or two, I thought.

So I hopped on her website, and found out that she runs these Writing Masterclasses for Gunnas – people who are gunna write, gunna do it one day but that day hasn't happened yet. Also on the website were details of the comedy masterclass I had just attended. Writing was the thing I wanted to do but there was something about the comedy that drew me in. When I was in my trough of depression, I completely lost the ability to smile or laugh and my usually sparkling wit deserted me. From the day I realised that I had laughed for the first time in months, I equated humour with recovery and mental well-being. So without further ado I'd booked myself a place, booked flights, and booked myself into Marita's spare room for the umpteenth time.

There is a huge lesson there in following your instinct and just doing it. I don't think I even asked myself *what if?* It just felt right and I listened to my inner voice. That quiet little inner voice that's trying to come out of me and that I know is my best friend ever because every time I listen to it good things happen and fear diminishes.

I think I have been fearful pretty much all of my life. I don't know how it came to be so. I don't know if I was born that way or if my upbringing made me that way. Probably a bit of both. I think that many of us are programmed to be fearful from an early age. Many years ago, back in the 80s when I was living the high life in London, the publishing company I was working for organised a bonding weekend in the Wye Valley. One of those outward bound kind of weekends where you work out how to get five executives across a river with a couple of tooth picks, a ball of string and a few fallen branches, propel yourself Tarzan like over a raging torrent, canoe solo down river on frothy white rapids and navigate through a dense forest in the middle of the night, avoiding booby traps and packs of wolves.

Well I loved it all. I breezed through all the tests. I was Miss Team-Spirit personified. I led by my quiet example of just getting on with things. I talked people into doing things they thought they could never do. I've always been quite physically strong and reasonably fit and I love the great outdoors. Out in the wilds of the Welsh hills I was in my element. Until we came to the caving that is. Not the sort of spacious well-lit show caves that are open to the general public. No, this exercise required us to wriggle, crawl and squirm through the narrowest of spaces into the deep dark earth.

I hate being underground. I imagine the roof or the earth collapsing on top of me and burying me alive, leaving me to a long, slow, tortuous, agonising demise. And I hate small spaces. I used to love all those Famous Five books where Julian, Dick, Anne, George and Timmy found themselves in yet another labyrinth of underground passages and rivers. And here I was on the verge of being able to live out my Famous Five fantasy.

But standing at the opening, which was no more than a tiny slit in the rockface, and realising that we were going to have to crawl through it, that I might get stuck underground and not be able to move and no amount of pulling or pushing would shift me and I would be left there to perish and never see another sunrise (what the fuck, I'm never up early enough to watch the sunrise), I started to shake, my pulse quickened a hundred fold and then, oh shame of all shames, I started to cry.

Standing there in my very attractive caving overalls and helmet complete with miner's lamp with the tears streaming down my face, I heard the instructor say, "Sue, you don't have to do this. You've done everything else, it's OK, you can sit this one out." But something made me stay, something made me do it. I continued to shake and cry for the first hour or so as we commando-crawled through the earth. Then gradually, my breathing slowed. I wasn't quite enjoying it, I wouldn't go that far, but I was less panicked.

After what seemed like a very long time, we stopped in an opening where we could actually sit up without bumping our heads, and the instructor told us to all turn off our lamps. We were going to experience what it was like to be in complete and utter blackness. We turned the lights off. No-one spoke. This wasn't the type of darkness your eyes adjust to, where shapes gradually appear and a hint of lightness can be detected amidst the blackness. No, this was the blackest of black. You couldn't see your hand even if it was right in front of your face and touching your nose.

We stayed like that for a while. And despite my discomfort, despite my anxiety about the very fact of being underground, for a few minutes I felt a beautiful sense of peace and belonging. I could hear my heart beating steadily in my chest. It was as if I could feel the pulse of the earth itself. The lifeblood of the universe was running through my veins. I was part of something big and mysterious and beyond comprehension. I squatted there in the blackness and I felt safe. I had faced my fear. I had crawled through the earth and now I was sitting silently and calmly in the dark, and all was well.

I had forgotten all about that time in the dark cave in Wales until very recently. Remembering it now brings me huge comfort. I sat quietly and surrendered to the blackness. I found my strength. I conquered my fear. When the time came to turn our lights back on, I was disappointed. I didn't want it to end. And as we crawled our way back to the light at the end of the myriad tunnels we navigated (there was even an underground stream we had to swim through – Enid Blyton would have loved it), I felt elated. I'd faced my fear. Now, years later, I'd come through a different kind of labyrinth, the labyrinth of my mind. I'd followed Ariadne's thread out of the maze, I was back in the light. Sometimes we need to take a leap of faith and run towards the fear so that we can open and expand rather than shrivel up and contract into ourselves.

> *I knew that if I allowed fear to overtake me, my journey was doomed. Fear, to a great extent, is born of a story we tell ourselves ... and so I chose to tell myself a different story ... I decided I was safe. I was strong. I was brave. Nothing could vanquish me.*
>
> ~ **Cheryl Strayed,** *Wild*

Chapter 32
BEYOND BLUE

Shut the door, change the record, clean the house, shake off the dust. Stop being who you were and change into who you are.

~ **Paul Coelho**

Over the last few years my ironing hasn't improved one iota but my approach to life has been transformed. Once I was through the worst of my depression I set about connecting with a part of myself I thought I had lost – my inner child, my soul, my spirit. I wanted to find out what peace and clarity felt like. Instinctively I knew the only way to change my life was to change my choices, my thoughts and my actions. I have come a long way but I am still learning, my story is still unfolding, my journey will continue.

So what have I learned? That depression and anxiety are not a life sentence. They are common, treatable conditions and absolutely nothing to be ashamed of. That with patience, persistence and determination you can find your way out of the darkness and begin to live a life that is fuller, more joyful and more meaningful than before. That people who have experienced depression and anxiety can contribute just as well as anyone else to the world of work. That I love and I am loved, and that I have amazing friends the world over.

I have learned that despite war and unrest and famine and displacement, the world is filled with beauty and we all need to tune in more to the restorative and healing power of nature. That we need to follow our passions and seek out the things we enjoy and that make our hearts sing. That we all have the power to create inside of us; we just need to dig deep sometimes in order to find our own special talents and gifts. That travel with intention does indeed broaden the mind, alter our perspective and allow new horizons to unfold. That in exploring our spiritual side we move beyond ourselves and our egos.

I have learned that while grief and suffering and loss shape our lives, they neither define us nor prevent us from experiencing great joy. I have learned that if I am not there for myself I cannot possibly be there for everyone else, and I have learned that I cannot be all things to all people at any given time. I have learned that overscheduling is not good for me and that I must take time out to replenish and refresh my spirit and care for myself along the way. I have learned that working when we are drained and exhausted is never a good thing. I have learned that if I try to please others all the time I may very well lose myself in the process.

I have learned that laughter is very often the best medicine and that the best comedy is often born out of misfortune and survival and helps us to deal with our own inadequacies. I have learnt that the quest to fill our bank balances and swell our superannuation funds is not as important as doing the things we love and spending time with the people we love. I have learned that being busy is not an indication of either my happiness or my worth as a human being. I have learned that getting one hundred 'likes' on Facebook does not make me more likeable. I have learned that there are lots of things I still want to, and can do in my remaining time on this earth.

I have learned to trust and listen to my intuition, my gut instinct, even if I am sometimes afraid. Had I not listened to my intuition I wouldn't have left my job, I wouldn't have travelled to Kerala and walked part of the Camino, I wouldn't have jumped on a plane to attend a comedy masterclass and a self-publishing workshop. If I hadn't followed my intuition, I wouldn't be sitting here today writing the last chapter of this book. Good things happen when I follow my instinct. If I ignore that gnawing feeling in my stomach that tells me something isn't right, no good ever comes of it. I have learned that exercise always makes you feel better, every time, no exceptions. I have learned that online interaction is no substitute for real-life communication.

I have learned that as soon as I stepped off the relentless treadmill I was on, time became my friend, my companion, not my enemy and I began to stop, to stare, to listen, to observe, to reflect, to breathe and to thrive. I have learned that holding on to past hurts, grudges and betrayals serves no purpose and will eat you up inside. I have learned that while it is important to clear out your metaphorical pantry and get rid of all the stuff that is past its use-by date, sometimes the past can help us to understand who we are and why we act as we do. I have learned that I can choose how I want to live the rest of my life.

I am learning to accept my imperfectly human self. I am learning to have less reaction to other people's dramas and other people's poison. I am learning to be more mindful and in tune with my thoughts, feelings, body, and environment. I am learning to savour the moment without feeling constantly rushed and preoccupied with what needs to be done next. I am learning to appreciate what peace and clarity feel like, to stay connected to my body, mind and spirit and listen to the signals they send me. I am learning not to fret so much about what other people will think and to have more confidence in myself.

I am learning to be proud of myself, to sometimes stop and remind myself that this year I have taught French in several schools, worked on various curriculum projects and made new and strong connections with fellow experts in my field; I have given twelve presentations at community and corporate events to raise awareness about mental heath; I have travelled to France and England and Ireland to spend time with some very dear friends and family; I have pursued my love of writing, travel and photography; I have delighted in the company of my husband and the two beautiful young men my boys have become; I have found time to exercise each day, to make stronger and deeper connections with my friends in Perth, to walk along the beach at sunset at least once a week, to share food and wine with friends and family, to sit on my yoga mat and breath in the silence. Not bad for a worthless failure who saw no point in existence three years ago.

I have realised that we are on this earth for such a short time; I want my heart to sing for as much of that time as possible and I want to do what I can to reach out and help others. I have discovered that every problem carries the seeds of opportunity to learn and grow and simply be happy to be alive. I wrote this short verse in a perfect moment when my heart was singing.

Clarity

Embrace possibility
Banish the doubt
Reject negativity
Let your words out
In the space between moments
All becomes clear
No more anxiety
A life beyond fear

Epilogue

August 2016

It is one of those perfectly-textured evenings towards the end of winter, when the sky is layered with blue and pink and purple and orange, and the clouds are aflame for a time with bursts of fiery red. I get in the car and drive the way I have driven a thousand times before, down the hill, left at the lights, turn right onto the beach road, pull up at my spot and get out of the car. The air is still apart from a gentle breeze, a remnant of the morning's stormy weather. I inhale with deep cleansing breaths. I am thinking of nothing in particular. With bare feet I walk down the beach track, the soft cold sand beneath my soles alerting my senses to the wonders of the beach on a winter's evening. I look up and down the shoreline, as if seeing this familiar sight for the first time. I scan the horizon, dotted with ships coming and going, off to some far flung land to deliver their goods or approaching their destination at the port of Fremantle.

I put down my towel and begin to walk. I walk past solitary fisherman casting their lines hopefully into the dusky sea. I walk past animated couples, discussing their latest renovation project, or a new job offer, or how to deal with an awkward family lunch on Sunday or any manner of things that clutter our too-complicated lives. I smile and say hello as people pass me by, making them look up, slightly startled, from the conversation that had been so engrossing them.

I begin to run. I laugh, I jump, I skip, I sing, I dance. I think of nothing in particular. I slow down as I reach the groyne, step up onto one of the rocks and sit for a while, gazing into the gradually diminishing light. I think about nothing in particular. I get up and walk briskly back to my spot. Bracing myself slightly, I strip down to my bathers and run to the sea. I immerse myself quickly amongst the waves, exclaiming as the cold envelops me but delighting at the same time in this life-affirming ritual. I splash around for a while. I lie in the shallow water and let the waves wash over me as I watch the sun finally sink behind the horizon, a distant ship outlined against the exotic orange glow.

I run back to my towel and swaddle myself in its warmth. I dress again, adding layers and my favourite scarf, and sit crossed legged for a while at the edge of the dunes. I feel swathed in light and love and filled with a deep, deep sense of peace. Every inch of my skin tingles, my body now clothed and warm after the cold of the ocean.

I gaze all around me, and above to the twilight sky where the first stars are beginning to twinkle. I watch as the blue of the sky deepens and more stars appear, and I feel part of something bigger than I could ever begin to comprehend. I think of nothing in particular. For a second or two I catch a glimpse of pure consciousness. I feel exhilarated yet calm, centred and connected. I give thanks to the universe. I am here, I am well, I am breathing, I am alive.

THE END

Acknowledgements

There are so many people who have contributed to this book simply by being in my life. In particular, thanks are owed to my dear friend Julia Stuart, New York Times bestselling author and award winning journalist, for being such an inspiration and for telling me that I just had to sit down at my computer and write.

Thank you to Julie Postance, for showing me through her workshop that I could actually make this happen and for her subsequent guidance, and to Catherine Deveny, for writing the book that finally demystified the writing process for me, and for Gunnas. To Rachel Berger, for telling me to stop being such a scaredy cat and to my editor, Amanda, many thanks.

To Dr Sophie Henshaw, for helping me find my voice and believe in myself again. To the friends I made in Kerala, in particular Janelle, Shayne, Jen, Gaye and Maree, for helping me be brave. To my fellow pilgrims on the Camino, thank you for walking by my side. To all my friends on the other side of the world, words cannot express what you mean to me. Thank you for the many decades of friendship. To Marita for giving me a home from home in Melbourne and for being an amazing friend, thank you. To KB for being there at just the right time.

Thank you to the very talented Jamie Ambrose, for showing an interest and being the first person to read part of my manuscript. To Samille Mitchell, Rhianna King and

Julie Hosking, thank you for your support and encouragement and for being such inspiring women.

To Julie Baker, thank you for lighting the spark, fanning the flame and for your unwavering belief in me. To Sarah Gamble, for your kindness, healing hands and gentle wisdom, thank you.

Finally, thank you to Pam and Richard for their love and support. To my beautiful boys, Daniel and Ben, for inspiring me every day, and to Ian for his endless love and patience and for giving me the time and space to follow my heart.

SUE TREDGET
AUTHOR | SPEAKER | TRAVELLER | TEACHER

Sue Tredget began writing several years ago when she took a year off to replenish her spirit after experiencing some troubled times. The thoughts and reflections she had begun documenting during that year turned into this very personal memoir of her journey through depression and anxiety.

On completing *Changing Lightbulbs*, Sue wrote the companion book, *Transformation: a collection of poems to heal and replenish the spirit*. In writing both prose and poetry Sue discovered the healing power of creative expression, and was able to gain the clarity and insight needed to make peace with the past and move beyond grief, loss and despair towards a more joyful future.

Sue is also a language teacher and the author of the children's picture book series, *My Colour Collection*. She grew up in Northern Ireland and now lives in Perth, Western Australia.

www.suetredget.com

www.ingramcontent.com/pod-product-compliance
Lightning Source LLC
Chambersburg PA
CBHW052015290426
44112CB00014B/2250